adventures
IN GOD'S
COUNTRY

31 Outdoor Devotions

Chuck McAlister

BARDIN&MARSEE
PUBLISHING

A Melcher Media
DuraBook™

BARDIN & MARSEE PUBLISHING
Birmingham, Alabama 35209
www.bardinmarseepublishing.com

ISBN-13: 978-0-9792394-2-7
ISBN-10: 0-9792394-2-7

Printed in China

Cover Design and Layout: Bardin Design

The illustrations in this book are composites of real situations and are included with the permission of the persons involved. Any resemblance to people living or dead is coincidental.

ACKNOWLEDGEMENTS

Growing older has caused me to come to realize the value of relationships and teamwork in the accomplishment of tasks that we could never fully do alone. As with nearly everything I do, this book would not have happened without teams of dedicated people.

To the team at Bardin & Marsee Publishing, I count it such a privilege to be a part of your family and look forward to the very many years and fruitful opportunities that lie ahead.

To the board of Promise of Hope Ministries – Sherril Schroeder, Bill Bledsoe, Ralph Ohm, and Russell Kennedy – thank you for believing in me and helping me to be my best, for continuing to press me and to pray for me during the good times and the rough. You guys have always been there and that means more than you'll ever know.

To the *Adventure Bound Outdoors* (ABO) team, it's such a privilege to do what we do together. Rob Snider, thank you for your able leadership; Terry Horton, for the passion you have for ABO; Bobby Martin and Chuck Myers, thank you for sacrificing personally in so many ways to ensure that the ministry of ABO continues to reach people in unprecedented numbers. You have kept ABO alive. Thank you for having a heart for ministry.

To the church at Crossgate Center, thank you for being an awesome church that's not afraid to embrace the gifts and the passion that God gives us to be ourselves and to reach outside the box to touch others' lives. I am so thankful for the privilege of being your pastor.

To my assistant, Stephanie, you are one of the great blessings in my life. Thank you for keeping me on track and on time.

To my family, one of the greatest teams of all. To my son, Chris, God has great things in store for you. You are just beginning to realize all the potential that is still ahead of you. To my son, Jeff, thank you for continuing to lend adventure to our lives. To my wonderful daughter-in-law, Brandi, thank you for bringing a wonderful heart of love to our family and for teaching our granddaughters to love Jesus like you do. To my wife, Janice, you're the best friend a person could ever have. Thank you for being so quick to embrace the adventure of life with me. I love you now and always. We make a great team.

TABLE OF CONTENTS

PREFACE

For years, I have loved the outdoors: the majesty of snow covered peaks, the persistence of a stream rushing its way to the ocean, the ominous gathering of a storm in the distance, the quiet simplicity of a walk in the woods, the peaceful feeling of gazing at a cobalt blue sky, the awe of watching a massive buck move stealthily through the forest, or the explosion of a cackling pheasant as it moves skyward. I am more alive outdoors than anywhere else. Countless numbers of people who pursue the adventure of the outdoors share this sentiment. What causes that response?

I think Job, in the Bible, answers that question best. He was struggling. He had lost everything, even his health, when his so-called friends showed up and began to criticize him. Job fired back:

> But now ask the beasts and they will teach you; and the birds of the air, and they will tell you; or speak to the earth, and it will teach you; and the fish of the sea will explain to you. Who among all these does not know that the hand of the Lord has done this, in whose hand *is* the life of every living thing, and the breath of all mankind. (Job 12:7-10)

The outdoors draws us because that is where we can get in touch with something, or Someone, much bigger than ourselves. This book helps identify some of the ways in which the Lord, who has created all, makes Himself Known. Whether God gives us glimpses of Himself in the helplessness of a new born fawn, the complex communication system of a calling crow, or the breathtaking panorama of a giant mountain, we should recognize that God has done all this, and He waits to take you on exciting adventures in His country. I hope this book helps.

Sincerely His,

Chuck McAlister

adventures

IN GOD'S

COUNTRY

31 Outdoor Devotions

SOME CALL IT MOTHER NATURE

Job 12:7-10

But ask the animals, and they will teach you, or the birds of the air, and they will tell you; or speak to the earth, and it will teach you, or let the fish of the sea inform you. Which of all these does not know that the hand of the LORD has done this? In his hand is the life of every creature and the breath of all mankind. (NIV)

Some call it Mother Nature. Some call it the great outdoors. Regardless of what you call it, if you spend much time outside, you'll quickly notice that the fingerprint of God is unmistakably on creation.

Whether you're seated on a deer stand at dawn, cutting across a smooth lake getting ready for a day of fishing, or watching a mountainside for an elusive elk, you're faced with the realization that there is no way any of this could have happened by accident. Behind it all, there had to be someone who put it together.

Well, there is! There is a God, and He put His fingerprint on all of creation. He didn't do it just to impress us with who He is. He did it to proclaim His glory.

That means we can learn some powerful lessons about life from creation, from the beauty, the majesty, and the wonder of the great outdoors–the adventure of being out in God's world. With the scriptures as its backdrop, creation becomes a laboratory for teaching us the most valuable lessons about life and what really does matter.

We often learn some of these lessons in the most unusual ways. Recently I ran across a passage of scripture that spoke to me. Job 12:7-10 says,

> "But ask the animals, and they will teach you, or the birds of the air, and they will tell you; or speak to the earth, and it will teach you, or let the fish of the sea inform you. Which of all these does not know that the hand of the Lord has done this? In his hand is the life of every creature and the breath of all mankind." (NIV)

Even the animals know that they were made by God. How foolish we become when we go about our busy lives forgetting God, relegating Him to the back of our lives as if He just doesn't matter.

The outdoors grabs our attention. As we stand in the majesty of creation, it tells us that there are more important things in life than busy schedules or that last deadline. For all our time-saving devices and technology, we're still a stressed, overwrought, busy people, who, at times, find it hard to put all the pieces of an overwhelming schedule together. That's why I like the outdoors. There's something about getting back to the simple things, distilling life back to its basics, and stepping out of the daily routine that causes us to see what's really important.

Take your family; see God's fingerprint for yourself.

We get so wrapped up in our schedules that we forget what matters. Perhaps it's time you took a break and went back to the great outdoors. Take your family; see God's fingerprint for yourself. Find out how important He is to you, and you just might find out how important you are to Him. The great message of creation is that you matter to God.

In fact, the Bible even tells us in Romans 1:20, "For since the creation of the world, God's invisible qualities–his eternal power and divine nature–have been clearly seen, being understood from what has been made, so that men are without excuse" (NIV). In other words, those things that seem so invisible about God when we're trapped in our routines, busily running here and there, can be clearly seen in what He's made. The message of creation is clear: God is real, and God is powerful! He cared enough about us that He created the great outdoors to show us how much we matter to Him. God is important to you because the pieces of life just don't fit without Him. But you're also important to Him. That's why He sent His Son, Jesus.

That's the truth…about what's important, in God's country.

THIRSTING FOR GOD

Psalm 42:1

As the deer pants for the water brooks,
So pants my soul for You, O God.

I believe God made man with an intrinsic hunger for adventure. As John Eldredge says in his book, *Wild at Heart*:

> Adventure, with all its requisite danger and wildness, is a deeply spiritual longing written into the soul of man. The masculine heart needs a place where nothing is pre-fabricated, modular, nonfat, zip lock, franchised, on-line, microwavable. Where there are no deadlines, cell phones, or committee meetings. Where there is room for the soul. Where, finally, the geography around us corresponds to the geography of our heart.[1]

That's why I like being in God's creation, the great outdoors. I feel free to be myself, to distill life to its most basic components. Please don't misunderstand what I'm saying. I never want to imply that being in God's creation is an adequate replacement for being in God's church. The time when I gather with fellow believers to worship

God allows me to publicly express those private worship times I experience during my time in God's country. During my private worship experiences in the great outdoors, I have learned some valuable lessons about life and those things that really matter.

Recently, while on a deer hunt, I was sitting by a water hole watching deer as they came to drink. While I waited, I began to think about deer and their desire to find water. Finding water becomes an obsession with deer when they are either nursing their young, fleeing danger, or just finishing an exhausting battle with another deer. Their thirst literally becomes their obsession. I began to think how the Bible even talks about this obsession. Psalm 42:1 says, "As the deer pants for the water brooks, So pants my soul for You, O God."

> Do I truly hunger for the presence of God?

As I began to reflect on God's Word while watching the deer, I had to ask myself, "What is my obsession? Do I truly hunger for the presence of God?" After leaving the water hole that day, that question continued to linger in my mind, like one of those familiar melodies that you hear and then hum for the rest of the day.

Several Sundays later, as I sat in church, we began to sing the praise song taken from Psalm 42:1. I felt compelled at that moment to tell God that I really wanted Him to have the priority in my life. The work that God began at the water hole, He completed in church. He seems to do that a great deal in my life–teaching me to draw closer to Him as I catch glimpses of Him and His love for me in the great outdoors.

That's the truth...about thirsting for God, in God's country.

GETTING OUTDOORS

Psalm 24:1
The earth *is* the Lord's, and all its fullness,
The world and those who dwell therein.

It seems that the scientific community has finally discovered something that many of us have known all along: being in the outdoors is good for you. In fact, new research seems to indicate that getting outside is an essential part of our development. Richard Louv, author of the book *Last Child in the Woods* states, "Outdoor experience isn't just something nice for kids to have. They have to have it."[1] Gordon Orians, Professor Emeritus of Biology at the University of Washington in Seattle, says that our love of the outdoors may actually be encoded in our genes. Being outdoors is fundamental to our well-being.[2]

Experts in early childhood development and neuroscience agree that the world of nature provides the primary means of necessary stimulation of all the senses. As a child becomes immersed in touching, seeing, smelling, hearing, and even tasting, the deluge of information to the child's senses creates a complex architecture in the brain. Throughout the rest of their lives, children will continue to build on the basic architecture they developed from the stimulation they experienced in creation.[3]

Have you ever noticed how blue skies and a bright sun with beaming sunrays dominate the drawings of small children? That's not by chance. Children see the world very differently than their adult counterparts. Up to and including the late teen years, the lenses of children's eyes allow more blue light to reach the retina. George Brainard, Professor of Neurology at Thomas Jefferson University in Philadelphia, states, "They see more blue, violet, and indigo."[4] That's why children feature those colors so prominently in their artwork. Exposure to the blue sky turns out to be a potential regulator of the human clock that tells us the difference between night and day and manages not only the rhythms of our bodies, but every organ within them. In short, God made us to experience His creation as a way of developing and growing into the potential that He established for us.

Children today, however, spend less time outdoors than any previous generation. In 1981, children ages six through seventeen spent an average of 100 minutes per week in the outdoors, according to surveys conducted by The Institute for Social Research at the University of Michigan.[5] By 2002, that time was cut in half to a mere fifty minutes per week spent in the outdoors. The notion of getting outside and spending time in God's creation has lost its appeal, and we will all be the worse for it. Whether it's making mud pies, walking down a country road, playing fort with their friends, or stalking that elusive buck with their dad or granddad, children need to spend time outside in God's creation.

The Bible has an interesting way of expressing this need.

Psalm 24:1 says, "The earth is the Lord's, and everything in it, the world, and all who live in it" (NIV). Simply put, the Lord is the Creator, and everything in creation is His. God planned part of our development so that we experience Him in creation. If we look carefully when in the outdoors, we can see the fingerprints of God everywhere, and these fingerprints are made by the same hands that molded and shaped each one of us. We have been made in the image of the God who made the great outdoors.

I have to confess, when I'm sitting in a deer stand watching a sunrise or gazing at snow-capped mountain peaks, there are times that I am awestruck not only with the majesty of God, but with the hand and the heart of the heavenly Father who could create such beauty for our enjoyment. Being in creation really does complete us in ways that we cannot fully describe. I'm convinced that creation gives us a taste of the experience of having a relationship with God through His Son, Jesus Christ. When I experience God's creation as a believer in Christ and one who knows Him intimately, I have an opportunity, through His majesty, to know His personal touch. And, after all, that's why God made what He made—so that we could know Him personally.

> Being in creation really does complete us in ways that we cannot fully describe.

Take a child into the outdoors with you. Experience once again the freshness of knowing that God is real, that He is powerful, and that He cares about you.

That's the truth…about getting outdoors, in God's country.

BELONGING

Hebrews 10:24-25

And let us consider one another in order to stir up love and good works, not forsaking the assembling of ourselves together, as *is* the manner of some, but exhorting *one another*, and so much the more as you see the Day approaching.

One of the greatest lessons I've learned in the outdoors has to do with belonging, and I learned it from one of the most unlikely sources–crows. Crows and turkey hunting just seem to go together for me, because crows always seem to be around when I'm hunting turkey. Crows have a complex system of communication. They can express many ideas such as: "Potential danger"; "Watch out"; "Here's a good meal"; or "You better get out of here." Those who study crows have distinguished over fifty various expressions related to the single syllable "caw." Most of the messages crows communicate to each other relate to feeding or protection. They have, however, a mourning call that expresses sympathy or concern for a wounded or dead crow. In fact, crows communicate so rapidly within a flock, that often several crows may gather and attempt to aid a wounded companion before the wounded one has even fallen to the ground.[1]

Crows have a system of relaying messages to one another and even assign certain crows as guards or sentries to watch for danger. When one of the sentry crows sounds a warning cry, the flock responds immediately. I'm convinced that the crows' dependence on each other is one of the factors that explains their ability to survive in so many different habitats. Each flock binds together as a cohesive unit by a high degree of cooperation and loyalty. Communication enhances their sense of belonging. Crows look out for each other; they help each other; they belong together. Everybody needs to belong somewhere. Yet, in a world that has become increasingly impersonal, it's easy to feel deserted, even alone.

Everyone needs to feel connected to someone else. God made us to be connected to Him and to each other. Everyone needs to be loved, and when people are genuinely united by the love of God, a sense of belonging takes place that affects us like no other connection we experience. People do need each other.

A few years ago, while visiting Northern California, I was privileged to see the giant sequoias for the first time. A park ranger told us that these huge redwood trees had root systems that were very shallow. However, they only grow in groves; you'll never see a redwood alone. They intertwine their roots so that when strong winds and storms come, they hold each other up. Their connection ensures their survival.

Crows and sequoias remind me that I was made by God not only to belong to Him, but to others. In many ways, when I am in the outdoors, I can sense God telling me, "You matter to Me; you're important;" and I find that when I gather with other believers in the community we call the church, I can once again hear God saying to me, "You matter to Me; you belong right here with My people."

I believe that's why God told us in Hebrews 10:24-25,

> And let us consider one another in order to stir up love and good works, not forsaking the assembling of ourselves together, as *is* the manner of some, but exhorting *one another*, and so much the more as you see the Day approaching.

God does not demand that we gather together as a church so that He can impose Himself on our schedule. Instead, as our loving Father, He gives us a directive because He knows that we need each other.

You and I were created for company. Remember, God made man and said, "It is not good that man should be alone," (Genesis 2:18), so God made man a companion. God also sent His Son to form for us a community, a family of people, to which we can belong. He called that family the church. We belong there.

The message of the crows and the sequoias, the message of the great outdoors, tells us that we can belong to God. And through His Son, Jesus Christ, we can also belong to each other. When you surrender your life to Jesus, you not only come to know the God who made you and the great outdoors, but you also connect with others who belong to Him. So the next time you hear a crow, don't just think about the flock that crow belongs to–think about God who sent His Son, Jesus, so you could belong to His family.

That's the truth…about belonging, in God's country.

DEER AND GOD'S PROTECTION

Psalm 119:93, 114

I will never forget Your precepts,

For by them You have given me life.

You *are* my hiding place and my shield;

I hope in Your word.

As we move into the spring of each year, we begin to see the baby animals that are born in God's outdoors. One of the most helpless of young animals is the baby white-tailed deer, or fawn. It has no claws, no fangs, and is incapable of running very fast for several days after it is born. The mother deer, or doe, does everything she can to protect her fawn from the constantly prowling predators that would attack it. She completely bathes her infant with her tongue, and as soon as the fawn can walk, she leads it to a place of relative safety. The young deer can stand within the first ten minutes of its life. It takes about an hour, however, before it can move its wobbly legs and follow its mother to a resting place.

For the next three days, the young deer remains practically motionless, its legs tucked underneath its body, its neck stretched out, and its head pressed against the ground. More than three hundred white spots cover the fawn's back, resembling the shadows cast on the ground by sunlight filtering through the leaves. The young fawn secretes no odor, and its spotted body blends in with the background, sufficiently camouflaging it from would-be predators.

Coyotes and other predators can quickly pick up the scent of an adult deer long after it has passed by. The interdigital glands of an adult deer deposit a waxy secretion that causes the scent of the deer's tracks to be one of the strongest in the outdoors. This is not the case, however, with the young fawn. Its interdigital gland does not begin to function until the fawn has sufficiently developed its running skills.

During the young deer's most vulnerable time, God has ensured its protection in a hostile environment. Predators can pass within a few feet of a young fawn lying on the ground and not even realize that it's there. Just as God gives protection to the young fawn, so He offers us His protection in the midst of an equally hostile environment. He does it by way of the guidelines and principles He gives us for how to live life. For example, there are times when God says, "You shall not." That is God's way of telling us, "Don't get hurt." When God says, "You shall," He's saying, "Here's how to be happy."

> God preserves our lives and protects us by His Word.

Psalm 119:114 says, "You *are* my hiding place and my shield; I hope in Your word." When you do things God's way, He provides your protection, and you have hope that you will not be overtaken by the predators of a hostile culture who would seek to destroy you.

Psalm 119:93 says, "I will never forget Your precepts, For by them You have given me life." God preserves our lives and protects us by His Word. When we apply His Word to our lives, we know that whatever happens to us will work out for our good according to God's promise (Romans 8:28).

I've come to the conclusion that every problem we face as a society could be solved by a return to God's guidelines: violence, crime, marital problems, substance abuse problems, and the list goes on and on. For us to truly know God's protection, we must know His Word. John 1:14 says: "And the Word became flesh and dwelt among us and we beheld His glory, the glory as of the only begotten of the Father, full of grace and truth."

Jesus is the Word of God; He is the Alpha and the Omega, the alphabet of God, so that He is the full expression of all that God is. Someone once asked Jesus, "What is the greatest commandment?" Jesus said, simply, to love God. That's where it all begins. You can't love Him if you don't know Him. Once you come to know God personally through His Son, Jesus, and you choose to live life by His guidelines, then you have the guarantee of His protection.

1 Peter 5:8 tells us that the devil is a predator and that he seeks to devour us. Like the young fawn, unable to protect itself from the predators that seek to destroy it, we must rely on Jesus for His protection from the predator who would destroy us. During your most vulnerable times, learn to trust God and His Word and, like the fawn, you too can experience His protection.

That's the truth...about protection, in God's country.

ENCOURAGEMENT

Ephesians 4:29

Do not let any unwholesome talk come out of your mouths,
but only what is helpful for building others up according to their
needs, that it may benefit those who listen. (NIV)

As any self-respecting duck hunter knows, especially in Arkansas where I live, the month of January is for hunting ducks. Only one ingredient makes for a successful duck-hunting season: ducks. And for there to be lots of ducks, two things are necessary: water and cold weather. Cold weather drives the ducks south from their feeding grounds in the northern states and Canada, and the water, at least in Arkansas, gives the ducks a place to stop. The blend of these factors results in a successful and fulfilling duck-hunting season.

In recent years, I've become more fascinated with the habits of ducks. I guess I just enjoy duck hunting so much that I want to make sure that we're doing all we can to preserve the duck-hunting experience for generations to come. One of the characteristics of ducks that has particularly intrigued me is the extreme protection that a mother duck offers her offspring. The female duck is careful not to reveal the location of her nest in springtime. She will very seldom fly directly to her nest. Only when she satisfies herself that the area around her nest is free of predators will she proceed to it.

Studies have shown that two to three days before the young ducks hatch, the mother duck does something very unusual: she listens for the faint peeping inside her eggs, and she actually communicates with her ducklings inside the egg. This ritual causes the young ducks to be familiar with the sound of their mother's voice even before they hatch. Experiments have been conducted to determine whether or not the communication the female duck has with her eggs is all that important. In cases where the eggs were kept isolated from the mother duck and communication was not allowed to be established, the ducklings would not respond to the mother or would require greater time and coaxing to follow her directions.

The mother's training of her young ducks continues for several months after they hatch. Small ducks stay close to their mother as she communicates with them, constantly guiding and instructing them. Studies have indicated that those ducks that hatch without the benefit of hearing their mother's voice and encouragement were less likely to survive the critical first year. Life is tough, and the dangers are extreme for a young duck in a hostile environment. That young duck needs all the help he can get, and it begins with the encouragement he receives from his mother.[1]

I'm convinced that most relationships fall apart because of the lack of encouragement.

The world, too, can be a hostile environment, and we need all the help we can get. The Bible tells us in Proverbs 18:21 that the tongue has the power of life and death. I'm convinced that most relationships fall apart because of the lack of encouragement. Marriages, relationships with our children, friendships, and even casual acquaintances are made or broken by how well we encourage each other through the words we say.

Have you ever been around people that just tear you down, who discourage you simply by what they say to you? People need our words of encouragement to build them up, to help them. The Bible tells us in Ephesians 4:29, "Do not let any unwholesome talk come out of your mouths, but only what is helpful for building others up..." (NIV). Rather than tearing others down by the words we speak, we ought to be building others up. When we should be helping others, many times we're hurting them. That's the great thing about the God who created everything. He cares about you so much that He chose to take the ultimate initiative in communicating encouragement to you. He sent His Son, Jesus, the Word [who] became flesh and dwelt among us (John 1:14).

Jesus is God come to communicate with us. He is the full expression of God, just as the alphabet is the full expression of our language. The 26 letters that we call our alphabet could express any word that we would want to say. Jesus expresses everything that God says to us. He is God communicating to us the love, the nurture, the guidance, and the direction that we need in this hostile environment we call the world.

The next time you are duck hunting or you just happen to see a duck fly overhead, remember that duck made it because its mother nurtured, cared for, and encouraged it. The next time you look in the mirror, remember that you, too, have someone who wants to love, to nurture, to care for and to encourage you. His name is Jesus, the Word of God, and He is speaking to you. Listen carefully so that you can learn to recognize His voice. It will prove to be the best protection you could ever hope to have. Besides, everyone needs encouragement, and God offers the best encouragement of all.

That's the truth…about encouragement, in God's country.

FLEEING AND RABBITS

2 Timothy 2:22

Flee also youthful lusts; but pursue righteousness, faith, love, peace with those who call on the Lord out of a pure heart.

On a trip to Alaska, I became fascinated with the snowshoe hare. We happened to visit at just the right time of year. It was the season between spring and summer, and we were able to see many of the snowshoe hares as their fur changed color from white to reddish-brown. For years, I thought this change occurred because of the onslaught of cold weather, but I discovered that it was the longer days of summer that caused the white fur from the hare's winter coat to molt out and to be replaced by the newer brown fur. This sounds like a complicated process, but it actually allows the snowshoe hare to be well camouflaged in all seasons.

While its ability to be so well camouflaged provides an important defense, the greatest defense of the hare is not its ability to hide, but its ability to run...fast and far. Hares are expert runners; in fact, they were made to run. They are different from rabbits, which are made to burrow underground and hide. The hare has longer hind legs, which give it the ability to accelerate rapidly and the capacity to maintain its speed for longer distances. Its rear paws are especially wide, which ensures greater buoyancy on the soft powder of freshly fallen snow. Legend has it that the Native Americans of the frigid climates of the North made their first snowshoes as copies of the hare's hind paws. Yes, the hare was made to run.

Perhaps you remember one of Aesop's fables, the one which tells the story of a tortoise that beats the hare in a race. The hare believed that no one could outrun him, so he took a nap after starting the race. He eventually awoke from his nap to watch the tortoise crossing the finish line ahead of him. While this story well illustrates the virtue of persistence, it also highlights the hare's capacity to run with great speed.

In short, the hare can expertly run from danger. His example provides good advice for the rest of us. 2 Timothy 2:22 says, "Flee also youthful lusts…" In other words, we can be hurt, attacked, or wounded by some things in life. These things can wound us or limit our potential, keeping us from being all that God wants us to be, and robbing us of the fulfillment of being all that we desire. Sometimes the best thing we can do is to not challenge these things, but just flee them instead. If you never light that cigarette or experiment with that substance–if you run from them, then they'll never trap you. Many situations become dangerous for us and call for retreat. Sometimes people or circumstances may influence us to do wrong, or maybe we are tempted through our own self-control, such as using that credit card we should have destroyed. We should not try to rationalize our way through these situations. Could you imagine a hare trying to rationalize with a wolf about why the wolf shouldn't eat him? I don't think so. One of the most skittish animals you'll encounter in God's country is the hare. It remains alert to any danger that could threaten its well-being. So should we.

One thing I've learned about life is that it's not only about what you're running from, but what you're running to. 2 Timothy 2:22 continues by saying, "...pursue righteousness (your relationship with God), faith (your relationship with the future), love (your relationship with others), peace (your relationship with yourself) with those who call on the Lord out of a pure heart." We should become, like the hare, an expert at running from anything that could rob us of God's best for us. We should run from the fear of setting up that appointment or calling that person we need to call to patch up that broken relationship. Run toward that situation that will stir you up to do your best, or run toward those people who will encourage you to be your best. This verse covers every facet of our lives and tells us what we must pursue in each of our relationships while we flee those things that can hurt us. Then we, too, can "call on the Lord out of a pure heart." Our lives will be much less complicated when we know what to run from and what to run toward.

The purity and simplicity of a life lived with your eyes open helps you know that you matter–that your life counts. A lot of folks find themselves busily running through life but not really going anywhere. You have the opportunity not only of fleeing that which is dangerous and damaging to your life, but of running directly to the One who made you. His name is Jesus, and He cares about you.

That's the truth...about fleeing, in God's country.

FACING LIFE'S CRISES

Proverbs 3:5-6
Trust in the LORD with all your heart,
And lean not on your own understanding;
In all your ways acknowledge Him,
And He shall direct your paths.

A father decided to take his young son into the outdoors to teach him the importance of recognizing our Creator in the world around us. He asked his son Luke, "Luke, who made the trees?" Luke responded, "Luke did it." His dad said, "No, now you know God did it. How about the mountains–who made them, Luke?" Luke replied, "Luke did it." The father went on and asked about the sky, the stars, and the ground. The response was always the same. Laughing, Luke would say, "Luke did it." Finally his dad just gave up, realizing this lesson would have to be taught another day. He helped his wife set the table and get the kids seated for dinner. He put Luke in his high chair and went into the kitchen to help his wife. When he came back, there was a glass of spilled milk in the middle of the table. "Ok," Dad asked, "who spilled the milk?" Little Luke immediately spoke up for everybody and said, "God did it!"

That's so much like us. Human nature says if anything good happens–I did it. If anything bad happens or an unexpected crisis occurs–God did it. When Hurricane Katrina pounded into the Gulf Coast of the United States, it all but destroyed New Orleans and the surrounding area, causing the recovery effort to last for months. We must face the fact that the devastation was overwhelming, and then we realize that this, too, is part of God's outdoors.

The intensity of the hurricane left a path of destruction creating a natural disaster this nation has not previously experienced. People lost their homes, their livelihoods, their loved ones, and some even lost their lives. It quickly became obvious that this storm was beyond man's control. But the truth of the matter is, most of us cannot control our lives. Sometimes God allows the shaking of certain things in our lives to show us what cannot be shaken.

> But the truth of the matter is, most of us cannot control our lives.

Hebrews 12:27 speaks of the removing of what can be shaken so that what cannot be shaken may remain. Verse 28 says, "Therefore, since we are receiving a kingdom which cannot be shaken, let us have grace, by which we may serve God acceptably with reverence and godly fear."

Hurricane Katrina was so massive that no one could control it. Many people wondered, why didn't God do something? Facing a crisis of this magnitude causes us to ask the tough questions...questions for which there may be no answers at this time. Proverbs 3:5-6 tells us to "trust in the Lord with all your heart, and lean not on your own understanding; in all your ways acknowledge Him, and He shall direct your paths."

When we face a crisis, we experience strong emotions:

discouragement, disappointment, frustration, loss, and even fear. But in the midst of it all, we can acknowledge our faith in God and not rely on our ability to understand what has happened because, frankly, some things simply cannot be understood. The secret of overcoming fear is faith in God and His goodness. We can realize that His kingdom cannot be shaken, and this can inspire us, even in the midst of an overwhelming crisis. The alternative is bitterness, a bitterness that will color every other part of our lives.

How do you keep from being bitter when you face an unexpected crisis? Accept what you can't change, and by faith, focus on what's left…not what's lost. Faith is not pretending that everything is great when it's not. Faith is facing the facts and trusting God to see you through. Psalm 37:5 says, "Commit your way to the LORD, Trust also in Him and He shall bring *it* to pass." Trust God to help you, and He will.

It's a big mistake to isolate yourself when you're going through a crisis, even though that's our tendency. We want to get by ourselves, but you and I need the Lord and other people when we face a crisis. That's why you need a church family to stand with you, to help you. That's why we needed

We need God, and we need each other.

to provide assistance to those in the area devastated by the hurricane. We need God, and we need each other. Those are two of the most basic lessons I've learned during my time in the outdoors.

On September 11, 2001, our nation was struck by another devastating crisis. One news channel reported that a young man, asleep in a building across from the World Trade Center, was awakened by the explosion when the first plane struck the building. He got up and ran out into the street. A security officer told him, "Run west!" The young man took off running west. He saw another uniformed officer who told him to run north, so he began running north. He came to another officer who told him to run toward the water, so he began to run toward the water. As he approached the water, another officer told him to run away from the water, so he started running away from the water. Before he realized it, he had run nearly two miles, and he was back at his building.

That's one of the dangers of being lost in the outdoors. You can end up just going in circles. The world will have you running in circles if you only listen to its direction in the midst of your crisis. God alone can give you a clear direction to see your way through any crisis you face. Hurricane Katrina did not take God by surprise, and for those who are willing to follow Him, He will make a way for us to turn every tragedy into a blessing. Remember, "all things work together for good to those who love God, to those who are the called according to *His* purpose" (Romans 8:28). There is no crisis too great for our God to turn to good. Trust Him. He'll help you no matter what you're facing.

That's the truth…about facing life's crises, in God's country.

CHOOSING

Proverbs 11:3

The integrity of the upright guides them, but the unfaithful are destroyed by their duplicity. (NIV)

In my study hangs a set of antlers from a six-point buck I harvested over thirty-four years ago. I was a teenager, and the adult that I worked with decided to take me on my first deer hunt. My friend dropped me off at the corner of a gravel road and a busy highway. Not knowing anything about deer hunting, I didn't realize that he was putting me in a place that was not ideal for the harvesting of a deer.

I sat down in a briar patch as my friend walked back to his truck and drove off. Suddenly, one of the biggest deer I had ever seen leapt over a bush about thirty yards in front of me, stopped broadside to me, and turned to look at me. I quickly threw up my gun, shot, and watched as the deer ran away. I remember thinking, "How could I have missed that shot?" I didn't realize that many times you can strike a deer in a vital area, and it will run for several yards before it collapses.

My hunting buddy heard the shot, turned around and came back to see what had happened. When I told him that I had shot at a deer, he laughed and walked over to the spot where the deer had stood.

Sure enough, there began a blood trail. He followed it for about sixty yards down through the woods, and there lay my buck. I can't explain to you the exhilaration that I felt when I realized that I had, in fact, taken my first deer.

I've enjoyed sharing this story over the years because it demonstrates the unexpected twists that can take place when you're out hunting and the choices that hunters face every time they go out into God's country. I later discovered that there was a trail along the busy highway that was, obviously, frequently used by deer and had been ignored by the members of that particular hunting club. What my buddy thought was a poor position actually turned out to be a good one. Without my partner realizing it, I had been well positioned to take that deer.

Much of hunting involves choosing to be at the right place. In the same way, much of life is about making the right choices. We are what we are today largely because of the choices we've made in life. The choices we've made, in large measure, determine our circumstances and situations in life.

When God created man, He made man superior to all other creatures based on his power and privilege to choose. Our capacity to choose is more powerful than anything else we do in life. It is more powerful than prayer because, before you pray, you must choose to pray. It is more powerful than anything you do, because before you do anything, you must choose to do it.

We constantly choose, and we are the result of the choices we have made. God has given us the capacity to choose, and with that capacity we can bring peace, pain, joy, or sadness upon ourselves based on the choices we make. Someone has wisely said, "We make our choices. Then our choices make us."

You and I make choices every day that affect our lives and the lives of others. We've all made bad choices: we wait too long; we pay too much; we say the wrong thing, or we set up in the wrong place for our hunt. Some of us face tough choices right now. Some of us don't know it, but we will face a major choice tomorrow.

It was part of God's eternal plan that man have the capacity to choose, even in Paradise. God set Adam and Eve in the most idyllic setting imaginable: in a garden. God set the Tree of the Knowledge of Good and Evil in the garden to ensure that Adam and Eve had the opportunity to choose. Without that tree, there was no freedom.

Freedom is the opportunity to make choices. Freedom gives us the right to make choices. Use your freedom to make the wrong choices, and you lose it. Adam and Eve learned that lesson.

> Cowards follow crowds; the courageous follow Christ.

Proverbs 11:3 says, "The integrity of the upright guides them, but the unfaithful are destroyed by their duplicity" (NIV). Or to put it another way: James 1:8 speaks of "a double-minded man, unstable in all he does" (NIV). When you live with integrity, your integrity will guide you by helping you make the right choices. But those who lack integrity will be destroyed because of their double-mindedness.

The truth of the matter is that most people today are moral cowards. They are afraid to make the right decision initially so that they'll make the right choices later. It takes no courage to blend in with the culture around us. Cowards follow crowds; the courageous follow Christ. Cowards don't last in the Christian life–they wimp out. That's why you'll never make a difference with your life until you make the right choices. And you'll never make the right choices until you make the most important choice of all: surrendering your life to Jesus Christ. When you make the choice to surrender your life to Jesus Christ, you not only establish your freedom, but you secure your place in eternity.

That's the truth…about choosing, in God's country.

FOCUSING ON WHAT MATTERS

Proverbs 4:25
Let your eyes look straight ahead,
And your eyelids look right before you.

There's nothing quite like the excitement that accompanies the opening day of the white-tailed deer hunting season. All the scouting has been done, the preparation has been made, and you're ready to harvest the elusive buck that will soon become your trophy. Recent decades have seen a dramatic increase in the number of white-tailed deer, and subsequently, an increase in the number of deer hunters. By the late 1800's, the white-tailed deer population was near extinction in America. Proper conservation and hunting regulations have contributed to the resurgence of the number of white-tailed deer.[1]

In May or June, the does have their young, usually twins, but three offspring are not uncommon. Fifty-one percent of the fawns born are bucks, or male deer. Over a ten-year period, a doe and her offspring can produce as many as 130 animals. Young deer grow rapidly on their mother's milk. The deer's milk contains twice the solids and three times the fat and protein of milk from a Jersey cow. Drinking this rich milk causes the fawn to quadruple in weight in a month, and it reaches 150-300 pounds once it has fully matured. The white-tailed deer lives an average of ten years. With few natural predators, deer hunting becomes essential to keep the deer population healthy and in check.

Anyone who has hunted deer knows that extreme measures must be taken to mask any and all scents because of the tremendous sense of smell possessed by the white-tailed deer. Products are available to remove everything from the smell of laundry detergent to the human scent. Care must also be taken to properly camouflage your position from the keen eyesight of the deer. Deer possess a remarkable ability to focus on both nearby and distant objects at the same time. This allows a deer to concentrate on what it's eating and to keep a watchful eye for danger. Many a hunter has blown an opportunity to bag a trophy deer because he was too conspicuous in his movements.

Because the eyes of the deer are set high and spread wide apart, the deer has a field of vision that almost completely surrounds itself. The white-tailed deer truly is the pinnacle of multitasking, as it can watch the food it eats while it also watches for danger. One thing I've discovered is that human beings are not deer. While we like to claim great versatility in our capacity to do many things at once, the truth of the matter is that we can only do one thing well at a time. Quite simply, it's called the power of concentration, and anyone who learns it also learns how to be successful in whatever endeavor they may tackle.

Our tendency is to be so easily distracted that we fail to give attention to what really matters. Proverbs 4:25 says, "Let your eyes look straight ahead, and your eyelids look right before you." The Lord knew that keeping our focus would not be easy in a world filled with so many distractions. In fact, keeping your focus on what matters becomes the most important ingredient in having a life that makes a difference.

So how do we know what matters? We let God tell us. Matthew 6:33 says, "But seek first the kingdom of God and His righteousness, and all these things shall be added to you." Obviously, seeking God's kingdom and His will becomes our most important consideration and should be the focus of our lives. Or, as the writer of Hebrews says, in Hebrews 12:2, by "…looking unto Jesus, the author and finisher of *our* faith…" we can run this race called life.

God says when He is our focus, when we look to Jesus, He will take care of everything else. It's so easy at times to take matters into our own hands because we don't think God is moving fast enough. We also like to keep our options open. What happens if God doesn't come through or if He doesn't do something exactly the way we think He should? Then we need to have a backup plan, or so we think. Your trust in God is not complete, and your focus on Jesus is not total, until you have no backup plan on which to depend. That is when you're living by faith—a faith that is focused and practices the power of concentration.

Nothing can stop a person who understands the power of concentration, much like a light focused and concentrated into a laser. Making a commitment of your life to Jesus Christ and surrendering control of the daily decisions of your life to Him keeps you focused on

> Your trust in God is not complete, and your focus on Jesus is not total, until you have no backup plan on which to depend.

His will and enjoying His presence. What are you focused on? Don't answer that question too quickly by saying what you think you should say. Two things determine your focus: where you spend your time and how you spend your money. Your calendar and your checkbook tell the true story of your life. They demonstrate both the up-close and extended focus of your life.

Maybe you need to do an honest assessment of where you focus most of your time and money. Then you'll know the true focus of your life. If it's not Jesus, then it's time to make some adjustments so that, like the deer, you too can be protected from the dangers around you. It's all about focusing on what really matters.

That's the truth...about focusing on what matters, in God's country.

SALT

Matthew 5:13

You are the salt of the earth; but if the salt loses its flavor, how shall it be seasoned? It is then good for nothing but to be thrown out and trampled underfoot by men.

A company that is considering being a sponsor for *Adventure Bound Outdoors* recently shipped me two sixteen-pound rocks. I know what you're thinking: what do rocks have to do with a hunting program? Everything. This particular rock is mined sea salt from Utah. With over fifty valuable minerals, these salt rocks meet essential nutritional needs in the animals, including enhanced antler growth in the deer that use it.

The ancient Greeks first expressed the virtues of salt for animals. Early explorers in Africa, Asia, and North America observed animals traveling to salt springs or salt deposits to satisfy their ravenous appetites. Animals deprived of salt resort to unusual behavior to obtain it because they instinctively know they need it. Considerable evidence exists that hunters took advantage of this fact to lure and harvest animals by locating areas with salt and waiting for animals to come there. Now you understand what salt has to do with hunting.

The sodium and chloride in salt are essential for life, not only in animals, but in man as well. I know that salt has gotten a bad rap from those in health care, but the truth is the human body has a continual need for salt, or sodium chloride. In the body, salt separates into sodium and chloride ions, each with a different task. Chloride maintains the balance of water between the cell and its environment, and it plays a part in digestion. Sodium assists in regulating the volume of blood and blood pressure; it also facilitates the transmission of nerve impulses and is necessary for heart and muscle contractions. In fact, salt is the number one natural component in all human tissue.[1]

In Matthew 5:13 Jesus says plainly, "You are the salt of the earth..." To understand what Jesus means when He says this, we need to understand the characteristics of this important mineral:

(1) Salt has to be broken.

Salt tends to lump. Scientists call that the hygroscopic tendency of salt. Salt absorbs the moisture from the atmosphere and lumps up. That's why we put rice in salt shakers. For salt to be used, it must be broken, whether it has lumped together in the shaker or in huge layers of rock salt underneath the earth. Like salt, Christians also tend to absorb their environment. Before we can truly make a difference in this world, we, too, must be broken.

(2) Salt seasons.

Research tells us that 14,000 different smells exist, but there are only four different tastes: bitter, sweet, sour, and salty. All flavor comes from some combination of those four tastes. If we took away salt, there would be little worth eating. We use salt in nearly all food products, from baked goods and cereals to meat. Salt enhances the flavor of the food we eat. It brings out the best in our food. Animals are drawn to salt because they know they need it and because they like the taste of it. We, as Christians, must also bring out the best in others. Do you know how we can do that? By doing what salt does–we can add zest and adventure to life. Somehow, we have propagated the idea that being a Christian is boring or less than exciting. There is nothing dull about following the purpose God has given us. Do you know what happens when food is seasoned with salt? It creates thirst. We should make people thirsty for living the adventure of knowing Jesus.

(3) Salt melts ice.

Of the over 14,000 uses for salt, the largest single use is for de-icing highways. Salt lowers the freezing point from 32° F to -6°. There are no cold, frozen churches when we're being salt.

(4) Salt preserves.

Salt is used as a preservative. We rub it into meat to keep it from spoiling or being corrupted by bacteria. Before refrigeration, salt was the means of preserving meat. You don't salt something that is alive. You salt something that is dead to keep it from rotting. Jesus called us the salt of the earth saying this world, without His influence, is like a rotting carcass. We are the salt rubbed into the rotting mass to delay the decomposition and to save this world from falling apart under its own wickedness. We can't restrain corruption if our conduct is focused more on the things around us than on His kingdom. We should conduct ourselves in a way that makes evil ashamed to show itself around us. We are the agents of preservation. Wherever the salt doesn't touch, corruption takes over.

(5) Salt penetrates.

Salt possesses a tremendous capacity to exert a powerful influence. When placed on metal and dampened with water, salt will slowly eat through steel. It can penetrate the strongest of metals and eventually crumble them into powder. There is not an institution, a philosophy, or an argument that can withstand the relentless penetration of God's truth as lived by God's people, because our power to penetrate is not of us; it has been given to us by God. He made us salt.

In Luke 14:34-35 the Scripture says, "Salt is good, but if it loses its saltiness, how can it be made salty again? It is fit neither for the soil nor for the manure pile; it is thrown out. He who has ears to hear, let him hear" (NIV). In other words, if salt stops being salt, it's good for nothing.

Salt is not only an essential part of our lives, but without it we lead a flavorless life. Without Jesus and those who know Him, this world would be hard, dull, cold, decaying, and resistant to God's influence in their lives. The world needs us to be salt, and we will never fulfill our purpose until we are.

That's the truth…about salt, in God's country.

FRIENDSHIP

John 15:13-14
Greater love has no one than this, than to lay down one's life for his friends. You are My friends if you do whatever I command you.

In recent years, I have developed a love for pheasant hunting. I specifically remember the first pheasant that I saw in the wild. I was a soldier serving in South Korea, driving my jeep down a dusty road, when I came around a corner. In the middle of the road, about 25 or 30 yards away, stood a beautiful Chinese golden pheasant. I remember stopping the jeep and staring in awe at the majestic bird while it ambled across the road.

It so intrigued me that I did some research about pheasants and learned that both the golden and the ring-necked pheasant are indigenous to Asia. It's thought that the Greeks brought the first two pheasants to Europe. In 1773 a dozen pairs of English black-neck pheasants were released on Nutten Island, New York.[1]

It was not until 1881, however, that the first successful transplant of pheasants to America was made. The U.S. Consul General in Shanghai shipped twenty-eight Chinese ring-necked pheasants to the Willamette Valley in Oregon. The birds adapted so well to their new climate that, in 1892, Oregon declared a seventy-five day hunting season. On the first day, an amazing harvest of 50,000 birds was taken.[2]

By the early 1900's, pheasants lived abundantly throughout many parts of the United States, with the primary exception being the Southern states. The hybrid pheasant that exists in the United States today is a composite of both the English and Chinese pheasant families. The pheasant truly is an adaptable bird. It has learned to survive by its wits, elusiveness, and great speed.[3]

While I do respect the pheasant's ability to survive, I find great pleasure in pheasant hunting because it's practically impossible to hunt pheasants by yourself. It is more a team sport than just about any other form of hunting. In most of the hunts I've been on, we line hunters across the field and walk toward other hunters, called "blockers," who stand at the end of the field. As the hunters walk through the field, the pheasant run ahead of them, weaving in and out of the cornrows or the hedgerows, sometimes sneaking inconspicuously through the low grass, and even doubling back behind the hunters walking through the field. Sometimes the pheasant will even sit and wait until the hunter passes by within just a few feet of him.

Inevitably, however, as the hunters approach the blockers, there are enough pheasants between them that the fun begins. Roosters will explode from clumps of grass or cornstalks, cackling as they rise. It's enough to unnerve even the most experienced hunters, but it is great fun.

I've had some great times in God's country, making friends and hunting pheasant. It is imperative that the friends you make on your pheasant hunt are people you can trust. They must be well versed in hunter safety, as well as hunter etiquette. They must respect each other and have a willingness to yield to their companion hunters rather than show off or dominate all the opportunities to shoot for themselves. You can really tell a lot about a person when you take them pheasant hunting. In many ways, you can find out who your true friends are: those who are unselfish are separated from those who only look out for themselves.

True friends are hard to find. Many people today seem concerned only with themselves or are just too busy or too selfish to take time to be a good friend. Going into God's country together is one of the best

> True friends are hard to find.

ways to find or make good friends. It is also a great place to teach your children the value of honest, open, and selfless relationships.

Do you have a good friend—a good hunting or fishing buddy? Don't take him for granted. Proverbs 17:17 says, "A friend loves at all times." In other words, whether you're having a good day or a bad day, whether you've been easy or hard to get along with, a true friend will stick by you. In fact, a true friend will put you and your needs above himself and his own needs.

I learned one thing a long time ago: to have a good friend, you must be a good friend. The best friend, according to the Bible, is the one who would give up everything, even lay down his own life, for his friend. Jesus said it this way: "Greater love has no one than this, than to lay down one's life for his friends. You are My friends if you do whatever I command you" (John 15:13-14).

Jesus gave His life for you and me and then told us that we were His friends. Going into the great outdoors, I am privileged to catch glimpses of God's love in many ways: a sunrise that leaves me breathless, the rich variety of colors of the foliage on a clear fall afternoon, the brisk air of a winter day, and watching the snow cover the earth. These are all simple ways God says to us, "I'm your friend. I care about you."

God certainly does whisper His love in creation, but He shouts His love from the cross. It was there that Jesus proved His friendship for me when He took the heavy load of my sin and died for me. That is true friendship.

Pheasant hunting is a good place to make a friend. But to find the best friend you'll ever have, check out church next Sunday. The best friend you'll ever have is named Jesus, and He's waiting to show you that He died for you, that He really does care. He really does value you, and He really does want to be your friend.

That's the truth...about pheasant hunting and friendship, in God's country.

GETTING HOOKED

James 1:13-14

Let no one say when he is tempted, "I am tempted by God"; for God cannot be tempted by evil, nor does He Himself tempt anyone. But each one is tempted when he is drawn away by his own desires and enticed.

As the leaves begin to turn and our thoughts also turn toward the hunting season just ahead of us, a few folks still get out on the lakes and rivers in pursuit of their favorite species of fish. I love to get out in the outdoors, to enjoy the reflection of fall colors on the lake, spend some time with friends, and, whenever possible, catch a good mess of fish. Fishing, when done right, can be downright fun. There's something about making that cast in just the right place, dropping that lure right where it needs to be, feeling the fish take the bait, and knowing the battle's on.

There's another reason I like fishing too. It teaches us a lot about life. We all tend to respond to what we want, to our desires. It's a lot like a fish responding to just the right bait. I remember several years ago, I had an opportunity to go fly-fishing for trout on the Frying Pan River in Colorado. I remember how the fellow we fished with carefully selected the fly, threw it out, got no response, and then carefully selected another one, until he found just the right color and just the right fly. Then the fun started. I later asked my friend if the color and size of the fly had made all the difference, and his response was, "Absolutely. The fish only respond to the bait they want."

I've not had an opportunity to fly-fish too many times in my life. Most of my fishing has been with a spinning rod and lure, pursuing that elusive big bass. What is true in fly-fishing is also true in bass fishing–you've got to have the right bait. I've often imagined what it's like for that big old bass, quietly cooling himself in the water, when suddenly that spinner, plastic worm, or jig drops right in front of him. I can just imagine as he starts to sweat around the gills a little bit, looking at that thing which looks so much like food and then deciding that he wants it. So he goes after it. But he gets more than the lure. He gets the hook, too, and with the hook, he gets a lot of trouble.

In many ways, that's exactly how we get in trouble too. The Bible says in James 1:14, "But each one is tempted when he is drawn away by his own desires and enticed." In other words, we get ourselves into trouble when we respond to the bait that Satan knows we want. More often than not, we find ourselves going after something we want so badly that we don't see the hook until it's too late.

Have you ever wondered why they call it "hooked" on something–hooked on drugs or hooked on this or hooked on that? It really has to do with the fact that people go after the bait, not seeing the hook until it's too late. And then, before long, the very thing they thought was bringing them pleasure dominates them. The hooks of life are so easily concealed.

The best way to make sure that you stay away from the hook is to make sure you want what's right. Psalm 37:4 says, "Delight yourself also in the Lord, and He shall give you the desires of your heart." I like the way *The Message* paraphrases that verse. It says, "Keep company with God. Get in on the best." When we pursue God, the One who created us, who loves us and cares about us, the scripture says that He will fix our hearts so that we want the right things. In other words, He fixes our wanter.

Have you ever wanted something, only to find out when you got it that you really didn't want it at all? I imagine that bass, sitting up under that log, seeing that bait, wanting that bait, taking that bait, feeling the hook, and immediately wishing that he had never wanted that bait at all. There are many people who have wanted certain things in their lives and gotten them, only to find out they were hurt by them. God wants to protect you; He cares about you. He doesn't want you to get hurt. That's why He sent His Son, Jesus, to keep you from getting hooked on something that could, ultimately, destroy you. Satan knows the bait that appeals to you. Let God protect you. Let Him take care of you. He knows what's best for you. Then you don't have to worry about getting hooked.

That's the truth...about getting hooked, in God's country.

GO AHEAD; GET YOUR FEET WET

Matthew 14:30-31

But when he (Peter) saw that the wind *was* boisterous, he was afraid; and beginning to sink he cried out, saying, "Lord, save me!" And immediately Jesus stretched out *His* hand and caught him, and said to him, "O you of little faith, why did you doubt?"

At certain times of the year, I can't help but think about going fishing. There's something about getting out on the lake, getting your line wet, and just soaking in the beauty of God's country.

Every fisherman has his story about getting caught in one of those sudden storms that can so quickly arise when you're on the lake. Every time I hear those stories, or if I'm out on the lake and see a thundercloud gathering in the distance, I'm reminded of the time when Jesus's disciples, who happened to be expert fishermen, were caught in a storm themselves. The Bible talks about this in Matthew 14:22-33. Jesus had just sent His disciples across the Sea of Galilee when, at what the Bible called the fourth watch (which would be around 3:00 a.m.), the disciples found themselves facing the churning waves and strong winds of a storm.

Perhaps you've been in the middle of a similar situation. You don't seem to be getting anywhere. You're working hard, back bent to the oar, doing the best you can, and all around you it's dark, and you really begin to wonder if anyone cares about what you're facing. To make matters worse for the disciples, Jesus sent them into the middle of the storm.

Suddenly, Jesus appeared on the scene, walking on the water toward the disciples and their boat. That tells me two things: first of all, Jesus knew exactly where the disciples were; and secondly, the storm wasn't so bad that Jesus couldn't find His way to them. The same is true about your life and mine. Jesus always knows right where you are, no matter how difficult your situation may be. He can also find you, no matter how far away from Him you think you are.

There have been times in my life when God has allowed me to face what appeared to be an impossible situation. There have been times when I felt alone, and times when I thought that maybe He didn't know where I was. But often I've learned that He sent me into the middle of the situation so that He could join me, to show me that He could handle any problem I would face.

> Jesus always knows right where you are, no matter how difficult your situation may be.

Here's where the story gets really good. Simon Peter saw Jesus walking on the water toward the boat and immediately asked Jesus if he could join Him. Peter was venturing into a situation different from any other he had ever faced. John Ortberg summed it up well in the title of his book, *If You Want to Walk on Water, You Have to Get Out of the Boat*. As Peter began to walk on the water toward Jesus, I can only imagine the feelings he must have had. He was doing something that no one had ever done before. He was risking it all to go to Jesus.

The Bible says that he saw the wind, and he started to sink (Matthew 14:30). Peter was walking on the water and suddenly a wave slapped him in the face and, no doubt, he told himself, "This is impossible. A man can't walk on water." Peter simply forgot that everything that threatened to go over his head was already under Jesus's feet. And that's the problem with this whole story. I know what you're thinking. You're telling yourself, "Why should I have the faith to venture into an area I've never been before? Look what happened to Simon Peter."

You're right; it kind of spoils the whole story. It was so sad when they fished Simon Peter's body out of the water. James and John were crying, and John was saying, "I shouldn't have let him go." The funeral the next day was even sadder...that's not what happened at all! Peter's faith may have failed him, but Jesus didn't. When Simon Peter cried, "Lord, save me," the Bible says that Jesus stretched out His hand and caught him (Matthew 14:31). You and I will face many challenges in our lives. Our faith need not fail us, but if it does, and you belong to Jesus, He will not fail you. I don't know exactly how Peter got back to the boat, but there are only two possibilities: either by walking on the water with Jesus or by being carried in the arms of Jesus. Either one of those possibilities suits me just fine.

What's threatening to get over your head right now? What are you drowning in? A simple prayer, "Lord, help me," is all it takes for Jesus to be there for you. No matter how dark it gets, Jesus can find you. No matter how high the waves, Jesus can reach you.

The next time you're sitting in your fishing boat, look out across the water and realize that there will be times in your life when you'll feel like you're in over your head, and remember, it will never be more than Jesus can handle.

Just a precautionary note: I don't recommend that you get out of the boat and try to walk on the lake, unless you see Jesus standing there calling you to come to Him. Otherwise, have fun fishing and remember, you're living life at its best when you're putting your feet where Jesus says to put them. Go ahead; get your feet wet. He'll keep you safe.

That's the truth...about getting your feet wet, in God's country.

PROTECTION

1 Peter 5:8

Be self-controlled and alert. Your enemy the devil prowls around like a roaring lion looking for someone to devour. (NIV)

One of my fondest memories of early spring is listening to the piercing whistle of the bobwhite quail. Recent years have seen a marked decline in the quail population, so hearing the whistle reverberating across the meadows and fields has become a little less common. I have to confess that when I do hear a bobwhite whistle, it takes me back to my childhood, and I often find myself whistling back, just to see if I can get an answer, and many times I do.

In early spring, when the bobwhite begins to whistle, it indicates that the coveys of quail are breaking up, and the wonderful adventure of courtship is beginning. The bobwhite will soon find his hen, and a brood of small chicks will result. The chicks will spend the summer growing rapidly into adult quail. During the fall, the different broods of quail will intermix to form larger coveys. This is known as the fall shuffle.

Once the covey is formed, the birds take on the responsibility of looking out for each other. Quail have many natural predators. The camouflage coloring of their feathers and their ability to run rapidly through thick ground cover enhances their ability to protect themselves; but they also need each other. They need each other for maximum protection.

This is especially true at night when they're sleeping. Quail roost on the ground in an unusual way: they lie in a tight circle with their tails pointing inward. Seasoned quail hunters can tell by looking at the pile of droppings left by the roosting quail how recently the quail spent the night in that location. Quail roost with their heads pointing outward so that they can spot any potential predator that would attack the covey. If a predator approaches the roost, one of the quail will see it and flush, causing the entire covey to flush and possibly avoid danger. This alert posture helps keep the quail safe at night when they are most vulnerable.

Did you know that you, too, have a predator that is after you? The Bible says in 1 Peter 5:8, "Be self-controlled and alert. Your enemy the devil prowls around like a roaring lion looking for someone to devour" (NIV). In short, the devil would like nothing better than to disrupt your life and keep you from living the purpose that God has for you.

Being in creation reminds me that there is a God. Having come to know Him personally reminds me that I matter to Him and that He has a wonderful plan for my life. I've learned, however, that just as God has a plan to bless me, the devil also has a plan to hurt me. The devil wants us to be his victims. Frankly, the devil pursues you not because you're that important to him, but because hurting you lets him hurt God. The devil knows that if you can't hurt someone directly, then you hurt someone they love, and you've hurt them too.

You and I matter to God. Coming to know Jesus Christ personally by surrendering control of your life to Him gives you a personal relationship with God that the devil cannot take away from you. However, the devil knows that while he may not be able to rob you of your relationship with God, he can certainly rob you of the joy of that relationship.

> That is why being a child of God is not just a matter of believing. It is also a matter of belonging.

We still need protection from the attack of the devil after we have come to know God personally. That is why being a child of God is not just a matter of believing. It is also a matter of belonging. We are not only meant to live in relationship with God, but in relationship with each other as well. Ephesians 2:19 says, "Now, therefore, you are no longer strangers and foreigners, but fellow citizens with the saints and members of the household of God."

Did you catch that? We belong to each other; we are part of God's family. I need you, and you need me. The Christian life was never meant to be a solo act. We were meant to live in community, or a covey, with each other. God designed the church as our community of protection. The Bible does not tell the Christian to make it on his own. We need each other. There are challenges, pitfalls, and predators in this life that will blindside you or even catch you off guard, unless someone watches your back. That is what the church is for.

If you have not connected with a loving family of believers–a church, then you're missing the joy and protection that God has for you right now. Like quail, we need to be alert to the dangers around us, and we need a covey–God's covey, for our protection. The church is the body of Christ, "the fullness of Him who fills all in all" (Ephesians 1:23). Don't miss the protection God has for you. Find your place in His church.

That's the truth...about protection, in God's country.

FREEDOM

Psalm 42:1

As the deer pants for the water brooks,
So pants my soul for You, O God.

Recently, when I was fishing with a friend on a local lake, we
came around a point on the lake, and, to our surprise, encountered an
eagle just lifting up from the water, beginning its ascent above the
treetops. I watched in awe as the eagle soared higher and higher until
it was nearly out of sight. That wasn't the first time I've seen an eagle
in the outdoors, nor will it likely be the last. On those rare occasions
when I am privileged to spot an eagle, there is something that
happens deep inside me. In fact, it affects me in two distinct ways.

At one level, it reminds me of the scripture and God's desire for
me to rise above the challenges I face in everyday life. Isaiah 40:31
says: "But those who wait on the Lord shall renew their strength; they
shall mount up with wings like eagles, they shall run and not be
weary, they shall walk and not faint."

On another level, I'm also reminded of the wonderful blessing
that we have been given to live in a nation that affords us the freedom
to pursue our dreams, speak our minds, and live our lives without any

fear of reprisal.

Yes, I'm patriotic to the core. I'm thankful that our forefathers chose the eagle as our national symbol (rather than the turkey as Benjamin Franklin suggested). The eagle is a majestic bird; it commands respect. Our nation should also command respect, and it will as it recognizes that God's truth is what brings respect and freedom. Proverbs 14:34 says, "Righteousness exalts a nation, but sin *is* a reproach to *any* people." And John 8:32 says, "And you shall know the truth, and the truth shall make you free."

I am particularly moved to remember the men and women who are serving around the world in our military. They preserve the freedom that the eagle so effectively symbolizes. They deserve our most profound respect and our deepest gratitude for the sacrifice they're making to protect the freedom we have been granted.

When I celebrate the birth of our nation every summer, I am reminded that we would not have the freedom that we enjoy were it not for the supreme sacrifice made by so many. There are many who have given their lives so that we can be free. One recent Memorial Day, I stood at a national cemetery and looked at row upon row of white tombstones garnished with American flags. I could do little but stand in sacred silence, realizing that I was looking at the representation of hundreds of lives that had been given for the freedom I enjoy.

Years ago, I served in the U.S. Army and was stationed in South Korea. One bitterly cold night, I was on guard duty. Few people realize that North Korea is all that separates South Korea from the Siberian region of Asia, so it gets very cold in South Korea in the wintertime. The temperature that night was 40° below zero. I was literally shivering in my boots, as I walked my post. I remember feeling especially sorry for myself, wondering what I was doing there when many of my friends were back in the States enjoying their careers, time with their family, and just living life.

As one of my buddies came to check on me, he could tell I was down. He asked me what was wrong. I had begun my sob story when he suddenly interrupted me and looked me square in the eye. He said, "It's all for the sake of freedom." In that moment, I had an epiphany. I realized my job was very important. Let's remember, with deep appreciation, those who are walking their posts and serving their nation so that we can be free. It's all for the sake of freedom.

Years ago, our Savior, hanging on a cross, lifted His head, looked toward heaven and cried, "My God, My God, why have You forsaken Me" (Matthew 27:45)? He felt the full weight of our sin invading Him. I can only imagine that as the Father turned away, brokenhearted that His Son was taking the judgment for our sin, He must have thought, "It's all for the sake of freedom."

The truest freedom that you and I can find is the freedom that comes from knowing that Jesus has taken our sin and that we have received Him as our personal Savior. John 8:36 says: "Therefore if the Son makes you free, you shall be free indeed."

The cross, Calvary, the crown of thorns, the blood that was spilled, and the Life that was offered...it was all for the sake of freedom.

That's the truth…about freedom, in God's country.

HURRICANES AND STORMS

Mark 4:39-41

Then He arose and rebuked the wind, and said to the sea, "Peace, be still!" And the wind ceased and there was a great calm. But He said to them, "Why are you so fearful? How *is it* that you have no faith?" And they feared exceedingly, and said to one another, "Who can this be, that even the wind and the sea obey Him!"

I spent several days in the Gulfport, Mississippi, area in the aftermath of Hurricane Katrina, working with the victims of this terrible disaster. I was not prepared for the extent of the damage and devastation that I saw while I visited. During the years I have hunted and gone into the outdoors, I've witnessed many weather-related events: I've been caught in blizzards in Colorado while hunting elk, torrential downpours in Kentucky while hunting turkeys, and even blistering sun while hunting doves in South Carolina, but nothing prepared me for what I saw on the Gulf Coast as I surveyed the destruction left behind by Katrina.

An average hurricane could provide all the electrical power needed by the United States for up to four years. A Category 3 hurricane could not be sustained for one day by the energy of the combined nuclear arsenals of all the nations in the world. To say that a hurricane is a powerful force is an understatement. While in Gulfport, I actually saw a piece of a 2 x 4 that had been driven through the tire of a Jeep. That is raw power. In the Gulfport area, bricks were ripped from buildings; hotels, restaurants and houses were turned into piles of rubble and splinters; birds were drowned in mid-flight as the water clogged their upward-facing nostrils. It is believed that some of those who died were not only killed by flying debris, but were sandblasted to death by the force of the sands blown by the powerful winds. We would do well to remember that a hurricane is called "an act of God." There is nothing more powerful in God's outdoors than the force of a mighty hurricane.

While we were in Gulfport, I fully expected to deal with people who were angry with God for the losses they had experienced. Instead, I heard over and over again, "God has gotten my attention. Now what should I do?" In all honesty, not one person voiced their anger with God. One man who came to our feeding station had been in charge of the cadaver dogs. He had spent the day marking bodies on the beach, when he came across what he supposed to be the body of about a nine-year-old girl. He began to weep uncontrollably and simply walked away. He wound up in our tent just needing someone to talk to. He was facing his own private storm, and he needed someone to help him through it.

> We would do well to remember that a hurricane is called "an act of God."

We all face storms at some time or other in our lives. In Mark 4:35-41, Jesus sent His disciples into the middle of a storm. While it certainly wasn't as violent as a hurricane, Jesus did use that storm to teach His disciples and us how to have hope when we face the storms of life. I believe there are four things we must do whenever we're facing the inevitable storms that will arise in our lives:

(1) Remember the promises of Jesus.

In verse 35, Jesus tells His disciples, "Let us cross over to the other side." Jesus didn't say to His disciples, "Let's go down to the Sea of Galilee and drown." Had the disciples remembered what Jesus said to them–that they were to cross over the Sea of Galilee–there would have been no need for them to panic when the storm arose. There are 30,000 promises found in God's Word. The time to hide the promises of God in your heart is *before* the storm, just as Jesus gave His promise of crossing over to the other side to His disciples *before* their storm. What promise do you need to learn so that you will be ready for your storm?

One day at our feeding station, a small lady arrived with a friend. As they were eating their meals, one of our team members began to talk with her and discovered that she had lost both her husband and two-year-old child in the storm. What this lady said next both challenged and blessed the member of our team who was talking with her: "I'll make it. I'll be fine because 'I can do all things through Christ who strengthens me'" (Phil. 4:13). Because this lady was a believer in Jesus Christ, and because she had hidden the promise of Jesus in her heart, she was better prepared to face her private storm.

(2) Rest in the presence of Jesus.

Mark 4:36 tells us that Jesus climbed into one of the boats and then an armada of boats began to cross the Sea of

Galilee "...and other little boats were also with Him" (verse 36). Out of this entire armada of small boats, there was one that was distinctively different because it had Jesus in it. It was unique. When you surrender control of your life to Jesus Christ, He comes into your heart–He gets into the boat of your life. There's a very important lesson to learn here about the storms of life: the presence of Jesus in your boat does not guarantee that you will not face a storm. Remember, these disciples did not go into their storm because of disobedience but because they obeyed Jesus. They were doing the right thing. The question is not, "will you face storms in your life?" You will. The question is, "Who is in the boat with you?"

(3) Rely on the power of Jesus.

Verse 37 tells us that the storm blew up quickly, and the boat began to fill with water. Verse 38 tells us that Jesus was asleep, and the disciples came to him and said, "Teacher, do You not care that we are perishing?" This is the only place in all of scripture that depicts Jesus as sleeping.

Have you ever felt that Jesus was asleep during your storm? Maybe you've asked yourself the same question the disciples asked: "Jesus, do You care?" I can answer that question with a resounding "Yes," and I can prove to you that He cares. It wasn't the wind or the waves or the storm itself that awakened Jesus: it was the combined voices of those He loved. Jesus doesn't react to your storm; He reacts to you, because He loves you. Verse 39 says, "Then He arose and rebuked the wind, and said to the sea, "Peace, be still!'" Jesus can rise to any occasion, and He can handle any storm. The phrase, "peace, be still" can actually be translated, "muzzle it." Truly, our God is so powerful that He is greater than any storm you or I will ever face. We can rely on His power.

(4) Realize the priority of Jesus.

The priority of Jesus can be summed up in one word: *faith*. In fact, Jesus rebukes His disciples for their lack of faith in verse 40. But He says to them, "Why are you so fearful? How is it that you have no faith?" We should understand something at this point. Jesus didn't confront His disciples because they lacked the faith to still the storm themselves. He confronted them because they lacked the faith to believe that He could handle their storm. Jesus doesn't expect you or me to have the faith to handle our own storms. He does expect us to have the faith to trust Him to handle what we face.

Verse 41 says of the disciples, "And they feared exceedingly, and said to one another, 'Who can this be, that even the wind and the sea obey Him!'" It's interesting that Jesus did not rebuke this fear displayed by the disciples because this fear was produced by the calm, not the storm. This fear centered on the identity of Jesus; it was a reverent awe of their Savior, who could quiet the storm with the words of His mouth. They realized that they did not yet know all there was to know about Jesus. They had a lot to learn, and so do we.

The place to learn more about Jesus, more often than not, is in the storms, because in the storms, you learn to remember His promises, to rest in His presence, to rely on His power, and to realize His priority of faith. Storms can cause you to run your roots deep into Jesus, but you can't learn more about Jesus in your storm if He's not in your boat.

One Sunday morning, shortly after Katrina hit, I stood on a patch of grass next to a church that had been destroyed by the storm. A man in his late seventies and his wife walked up and stood on the sidewalk as I shared about how Jesus could help you in the storms of life. I led a prayer and asked to come forward those who prayed with me to receive Jesus as their Savior. I watched as, arm in arm, this older gentleman and his wife came forward, walked up to me, and the man said, "God has gotten my attention. I want Jesus in my boat." By the way, the man with the cadaver dogs was the first to come forward and get Jesus in his boat. Faith can be born in the storm.

That's the truth…about hurricanes and storms, in God's country.

LOYALTY

1 Corinthians 1:9
God *is* faithful, by whom you were called into the
fellowship of His Son, Jesus Christ our Lord.

As the fall of the year approaches, those of us who love the outdoors and who enjoy hunting begin to count the days until the opening of our favorite season. We're already checking out our favorite spots in anticipation of the exciting season ahead. It won't be long before the leaves will turn, the air will be crisp and cool, and the sounds of migrating ducks and geese will fill the air. Living as I do on the Mississippi flyway, I have had the privilege of witnessing the annual migration of some of God's most beautiful creatures: Canadian geese.

For years I have been fascinated with not only the beauty of these majestic creatures, but the one thing that makes them distinctive in all of God's creation–their loyalty. The Canadian goose is extremely resourceful, flying up to seventy-five percent farther because it flies in formation rather than alone. Its loyalty, however, is its most pronounced characteristic. The Canadian goose mates for life. In fact, if a goose is wounded, its mate will often remain with it until it is healed. I have heard hunters tell stories of shooting a goose only to watch its mate circle back, risking death itself, in an attempt to help its partner. If for some reason a goose can't make the difficult migration south for the winter, often its mate will stay by its side, facing the harsh winter with its partner. More often than not, both geese will die together as a result of the winter weather, while the one that is not wounded could have been saved.

The intense loyalty that characterizes the Canadian goose not only extends to its mate, but also to its young. While mature geese have few natural enemies, those geese that are raising their young have been known to take on a raccoon or even a fox to protect their small ones. Recently, I was reading an account of an unseasonably late spring snowstorm that came to the breeding ground of the Canadian geese. The snow continued falling until it reached a depth of three feet. As the snow melted away days later, an amazing picture of loyalty was revealed. Scores of dead geese were found still sitting on their nests. They had chosen to suffocate rather than leave the eggs they were protecting.

As I reflect on the intense loyalty of the Canadian goose, I am convinced that it is a reflection of our Creator's heart. When we talk about God, we have another word for this loyalty. We call it *faithfulness*. 1 Corinthians 1:9 says, "God is faithful, by whom you were called into the fellowship of His Son, Jesus Christ our Lord." I like the way *The Message* paraphrases this verse when it says, [God] "will never give up on you. Never forget that." Faithfulness, or loyalty, is one of God's greatest characteristics. In Hebrews 13:5 He says, *"I will never leave you nor forsake you."* Loyalty holds relationships together. Without it, marriages, families, and friendships fall apart. That is why loyalty is so important. When others give up and quit, loyal people are reliable and consistent. You can count on the steadiness of loyalty, and God shows loyalty to those who are His.

As I think back over my life, I am humbled by the intense loyalty that God has shown to me when I have least deserved it. His blessings and His grace have been there in spite of my fickleness and my foolish moods. He has been consistent; He has always remained loyal to me.

> You can count on the steadiness of loyalty, and God shows loyalty to those who are His.

During the cold days of the late fall, I will stand on the edge of flooded timber in Eastern Arkansas or sit in a duck blind, and I will hear the familiar honk and see the V-shape formation of geese flying overhead. At that moment I will pause, and, for just a moment, I will think about how fortunate I am to know personally the God who not only created the geese, but who created me. I will breathe a prayer thanking God for the many ways He has proven His loyalty to me, and I will once again resolve, in my own heart, to faithfully live for the One who cared so much that He sent His Son for me. Then I'll realize that's a loyalty I'll never deserve. That's why it's called grace.

That's the truth...about loyalty, in God's country.

GOOD SCENTS

2 Corinthians 2:15-16

For we are to God the aroma of Christ among those who are
being saved and those who are perishing. To the one we are the
smell of death; to the other, the fragrance of life… (NIV)

Most outdoorsmen anxiously await the beginning of deer season.
Some anticipate the start of bow season; others look forward to the
beginning of muzzle-loader or the modern gun season; the diehards,
who hunt all three seasons, are just ready to hit the woods. Regardless
of your preference, food plots are prepared, your favorite area has
been scouted, and the deer activity has been noted. The hunting
equipment has been readied, and you are ready to "get it on."

As an important part of his arsenal, every deer hunter carries
something to mask, or hide, his odor. I don't mean to imply that outdoorsmen smell bad, but after a few days at deer camp, that is fairly
well assured. Deer have a remarkable sense of smell that every hunter
must counteract, in some way, in order to have a successful hunt.

There are products to bathe in and to wash your hunting clothes
in so that you can mask the odor that we humans naturally secrete.
You can buy sprays, wicks to burn while you're on your deer stand,
and even bottles of deer urine to sprinkle around on the ground to keep

the deer from smelling you and being startled. To the novice this may sound like way too much trouble and way too much attention to detail. However, more than one hunt has been ruined when a deer has been spooked by catching a whiff of an otherwise undetectable hunter.

The sense of smell is an important part of being in the outdoors. Those who hunt with dogs, whether they are hunting upland game birds, rabbits, coons, or other animals, will attest to how much a dog relies on his sense of smell. Smelling is an important part of hunting.

Recently, I talked to a friend, and he showed me an old, tattered coat that had belonged to his father. He told me a story about how the coat had been an important part of a coon hunt that his father had taken him on. As coon hunters tend to do, they had gathered around the campfire and were listening to the dogs baying as they had finally treed the coon. The hunters went to retrieve their dogs, and my friend's father discovered that his favorite hunting dog was missing. They looked unsuccessfully for the dog, and they finally went back to the last place the dog had been. The father took off his old, tattered coat, laid it on the ground, and told his son they'd be back in the morning at sun up to check for the dog. Sure enough, the next morning they came back to that same spot, and there was the coat lying on the ground. Curled up on the coat was that old coon hound. He had come to the scent of his master.

We all have smells that are important to us or that trigger a special memory. Whenever I smell a certain brand of aftershave, it reminds me of my dad. Whenever I smell a hot coconut cake, it reminds me of standing in my grandmother's kitchen. The smell of sweat mingled with sawdust reminds me of my grandfather and the days I helped him on the job. We all carry a certain aroma.

II Corinthians 2:14-16 says,

> But thanks be to God, who...through us spreads everywhere
> the fragrance of the knowledge of him. For we are to God the
> aroma of Christ among those who are being saved and those
> who are perishing. To the one we are the smell of death; to
> the other, the fragrance of life... (NIV)

Do you smell like Christ? Do you carry His aroma? Do people smell Jesus around you? Those people that share with us a commitment to Christ will share with us the sweet smell of having died to self, the smell of death–but not the stench of a rotting corpse. To those who don't know Christ, we can carry the fragrance of life, the opportunity for them to see and know the benefits of eternal life from the aroma of our lives.

That brings up an interesting question: what fragrance does your life emit to God? In John 12, Mary bursts into the room and begins anointing Jesus's body with a substance known as spikenard. John 12:3 says "...and the house was filled with the fragrance of the perfume."

This was the fragrance of sacrifice. Spikenard was the substance used to pour on the bodies of those who, in Jesus's day, were being buried. It was said the substance would adhere to the skin and would linger for days, even weeks, until it was reactivated by a liquid. Then it could be smelled anew.

I can only speculate that as Jesus was being cruelly beaten, and, later, as He was nailed to the cross, the liquid of His blood flowed across His skin, and no doubt reactivated the perfume that Mary had poured on His body. As Jesus died, He smelled the lingering aroma of Mary's sacrifice.

What aroma does your life produce for the Savior to smell? Is it one of selfishness or one of sacrifice? Smell matters, in deer hunting and in life.

That's the truth…about good scents, in God's country.

SOARING

Isaiah 40:31
But those who wait on the LORD
Shall renew *their* strength;
They shall mount up with wings like eagles,
They shall run and not be weary,
They shall walk and not faint.

Several years ago, my wife and I took a trip to Alaska to celebrate our wedding anniversary. I had certainly experienced the majesty of God's creation in other locations, but I was not prepared to be as overwhelmed with the greatness of God's creation as I was when I viewed the Alaskan landscape.

One of the most fascinating activities that my wife and I enjoyed while on our Alaskan adventure was sitting and watching the eagles fish. For hours we watched while they would soar almost out of sight, or sit quietly in the treetops, until, suddenly, they dove toward the water, skimmed the surface and extracted enormous fish from the water with their talons. My wife and I had been accustomed to seeing eagles during certain months in central Arkansas, but we had never seen quite so many, nor had we seen them quite so close.

Watching these eagles reminded me of a story that I once heard about an old man who watched an eagle soar across the sky. As he watched, the eagle flew lower and lower, until, finally, its wings began to fold and flap. Suddenly, the eagle smashed into the side of a cliff. The man walked over, picked up the eagle, and there, clutched to its breast, was a snake. Biologists tell us that the only natural enemy an eagle has is a snake. On occasions, when an eagle lands in its nest, a snake may be in the nest eating the eagle's eggs. The snake will often attack the eagle and can destroy it.

Did you know the Bible compared those of us who are God's children to eagles? It says in Isaiah 40:31,

> But those who wait on the Lord
>> Shall renew *their* strength;
>> They shall mount up with wings like eagles;
>> They shall run and not be weary;
>> They shall walk and not faint.

In the original language in which this verse was written, the word for "wait" can also be translated "hope." This word literally means to twist weak strands into a strong rope, which tells us that our weakness can be woven together with the strength of the Lord, producing a hope that can lift us to new heights and allow us the benefits of soaring with the Lord.

Many times, however, we fail to soar above the circumstances and problems in our lives because of what we're carrying with us. We pick up habits or attitudes that could drag us down or even destroy us and our families. The key is staying in touch with the God who created us so that we can rise above the challenges that could so easily defeat us.

The scripture tells us that those who hope in the Lord will not only find renewed strength, but they will spread their wings and soar like eagles. Circumstances can get you down if you let them. Challenges can come from mistakes that you have made or injustices that have been done to you. You choose how you will respond to each of these challenges.

> The key is staying in touch with the God who created us…

A poster that recently caught my attention contained this message. "How can I soar like an eagle when I live among turkeys?" The condition of your heart determines whether you soar or not. The choice is yours. It begins with your attitude, not with your circumstances. God made you to soar, not to be grounded by situations that may have overwhelmed you.

Like the snake clinging to the chest of the eagle, we all face our share of situations and people who hold us back or weigh us down. Whatever burden or person is weighing you down, surrender it to the God who created you and sent His Son, Jesus, so that you could be free. John 8:36 says, "Therefore if the Son makes you free, you shall be free indeed." You can be free to soar like an eagle when the God of all creation has become your God through His Son, Jesus. Then the Lord will renew your strength so that you can mount up with wings like eagles.

Is it possible that you have forgotten just how great our God is? Is there something keeping you from experiencing everything God has for you? Today would be a great day to surrender your weakness to God's strength and find the hope that He makes available to those who trust Him.

That's the truth…about soaring, in God's country.

LITTLE THINGS

Luke 16:10
Whoever can be trusted with very little can also be trusted with much, and whoever is dishonest with very little will also be dishonest with much. (NIV)

Several years ago, I was winding up a week-long hunting trip in Colorado, and I was disappointed that I had not been able to bag a bull elk. I not only had a bull elk tag, but also a mule deer tag, and I thought that I would, at least, get a good-sized buck, even if I didn't get an elk. The hunt, however, had been unsuccessful. The mule deer season had gone out the day before, and I had not seen an elk to date. As dusk was fading into twilight, I decided it was time to head back to camp.

Just as I was walking along the edge of the woods, a movement in the meadow near the woods caught my eye. I immediately dropped to my knee and saw the largest buck mule deer I had ever seen, or hoped to see, in my life. My heart began to race. The deer was well within range, and the crosshairs on my scope were at exactly the right place. I had the deer tag in my pocket. I could pull the trigger, take this trophy buck, and no one would ever have to know that I had harvested this deer the day after the season went out.

I clicked off the safety and began to squeeze the trigger, when, suddenly, something interrupted me. It was a scripture verse, of all things, that I had memorized as a child. I tried to ignore it, but there it was, not just whispering but screaming its truth. It just wouldn't go away.

Luke 16:10 says, "Whoever can be trusted with very little can also be trusted with much. And whoever is dishonest with very little will also be dishonest with much" (NIV).

I couldn't believe that verse was screaming in my heart. Then I thought about my sons: what would I want them to do in this situation? Then I thought about my church family, my community in Christ: what would they think if they found out that I had made this compromise? Then I thought about my wife: what would she say? Then I thought about the Lord: what would He say?

I knew what He would say. He had already shown me His Word on the matter. Very quietly, I clicked my safety back on, lowered my rifle, and sat for the next fifteen or twenty minutes watching the biggest buck I'd ever seen quietly graze not more than 100 yards from me. My decision was made. In the scheme of things in the world, it was a small decision, but it was also an important one. That day I was reminded of an important lesson. Little things do matter; in fact, they are very important.

It's not the big things, the big decisions, that bring discouragement or despair or that destroy marriages, relationships, businesses, or even lives. It's the small things. It's those small decisions that we make. Song of Solomon 2:15 says that it is "the little foxes that spoil the vines." It's those little things that can undo you the quickest.

I was reading recently about a huge tree that collapsed not too far from where I was hunting in Colorado. It was estimated to be over 400 years old. Over the centuries it had been struck by lightning fourteen times. It had braved countless storms of tremendous intensity, and it even survived an earthquake that had devastated the region. What caused this mighty guardian of the forest to fall? What was it that finally destroyed it? It was a beetle, a tiny bug, just a little thing.

> It's the small, intimate details of our relationships and our choices in life that really shape who we are.

We think we build our character and trust with others around us in one big moment, by making one big impression. It's actually just the opposite. It's the small, intimate details of our relationships and our choices in life that really shape who we are. In fact, Jesus told us that we can greatly simplify our lives by making one small, but important decision: Matthew 6:33 says, "But seek first His kingdom and His righteousness, and all these things will be given to you as well."

Recently, I was reminiscing about my passing up that big buck, and I have to admit that I was thankful that it wasn't hanging on my wall. I believe it would have served as a continual reminder of the day that I decided to be dishonest in something that seemed trivial. I pulled down my *Message* paraphrase of the Bible and I reread what God had spoken to my heart that day:

> If you're honest in small things,
>   you'll be honest in big things;
> If you're a crook in small things,

you'll be a crook in big things.

If you're not honest in small jobs,

who will put you in charge of the store? (Luke 16:10)

Character really does matter, and it can be seen best in the small choices that we make in life. Maybe I'll take that big buck someday. In the meantime, the memory of the one I passed up will serve as a reminder that it's the little things, those small choices, that really shape who we are.

That's the truth…about those "little things," in God's country.

SURPRISE

Jeremiah 29:11

"For I know the plans I have for you," declares the LORD, "plans to prosper you and not to harm you, plans to give you hope and a future." (NIV)

One of the things I love most about being in the outdoors is the occasional surprise that happens to those who spend time in God's country. In the swamps of Arkansas, God provided just such a surprise when an ivory-billed woodpecker, thought to be extinct for more than sixty years, was sighted. At least seven confirmed sightings of the bird have now occurred, and a brief video of a male ivory-billed woodpecker landing on a tupelo tree has been captured. The ivory-billed woodpecker has a wingspan of over three feet and can stand eighteen to twenty inches tall. It is the largest woodpecker in North America and one of the largest in the world.

The woodpecker disappeared when the bottomland forests of North America were logged. Relentless searches over the last sixty years have only produced false alarms, until recently when the first sighting proved to be a huge surprise. I've enjoyed reading the news accounts of the experts who have been surprised and elated with the discovery of the bird once thought extinct. Those of us who have a personal relationship with God understand how prone He is toward surprises, and those surprises don't just happen in the outdoors.

In fact, God often moves us toward His will by the unexpected. We love surprises, and we hate them. The direction they happen to take us determines our reaction to them:

- "The doctor's ready to discuss the results of your test."
- "Congratulations—there are three heartbeats!"
- "Welcome. You're hired."
- "I'm sorry. It's not the spark plugs. Your entire engine is shot."
- "Get out a piece of paper. We're going to have a pop test."
- "Dad, Mom…he wants to marry me."

These surprises often catch us off guard, but they don't catch God off guard.

In 1980, the Pacific Northwest shuddered under the devastating eruption of Mount St. Helens. Forests were annihilated, rivers were choked, fish and wildlife destroyed, and the air poisoned. The predictions were ominous. Acid rain clouds would form; weather patterns could be permanently changed. But scientists studying the area were greatly surprised.

They discovered that the salmon had found their way back to their spawning grounds by following alternate streams home, some less than six inches deep. New plant life began to appear in the rich volcanic soil. Farmers were surprised to find that the nutrients in the volcanic ash would support years of future crops. New wildlife began to appear on the scene. All were surprised that what many had predicted to be a terrible devastation turned out to be a rejuvenation of the land.

The Bible is a conglomeration of one surprise after another:

- Abraham being told he would father a child in his later years.
- Moses standing on the edge of the Red Sea with Egyptians breathing down his neck.
- Shepherds awakened in the middle of the night by angels announcing the birth of Jesus.
- A confused band of disciples hiding in horror from the Roman authorities who took their Master.
- A cross on which the Son of God died.
- A tomb from which the Son of God arose.

All these were surprises to man, but planned by God. Nothing catches God by surprise. In fact, what appears as haphazard to man can, in fact, be God's orchestrated plan. The Lord says to us, "For I know the plans I have for you," declares the Lord, "plans to prosper you and not to harm you, plans to give you hope and a future" (Jeremiah 29:11 NIV). In other words, the process may surprise us, but the end result is in the hands of our loving Father. The cross certainly surprised the followers of Jesus, but God's plan was the empty tomb and His Son Jesus in our hearts.

Whether it's ivory-billed woodpeckers in the swamps of Arkansas or tests from the doctor, it really is all part of the plan of the God who not only gave us the great outdoors, but also offers us a life filled with His purpose and direction. Whatever you are experiencing that you think is a surprise could simply be God moving you toward His will by the unexpected. So remember, with a few of God's surprises ahead, the best is yet to come.

That's the truth...about surprises, in God's country

SIGNIFICANCE

Psalm 139:14

I praise you because I am fearfully and wonderfully made; your works are wonderful, I know that full well. (NIV)

Recently, I had the opportunity to fulfill a life-long dream. I was privileged to go fishing at a lodge in Canada with a group of fellow outdoorsmen. I don't want you to think that I'm a great fisherman, because I'm not, but I love any excuse that allows me to get out into God's outdoors.

It was a trip of firsts. I caught my first pike and my first muskie. We fished in an area so remote that it could only be reached by float plane. On the last day of our trip, we took a boat to the far end of the lake and hiked over land to another remote lake where muskie were known to be. Until that point, I had not caught a muskie, so I was excited about the opportunity.

After arriving at the remote lake, we cast off in some small boats and began fishing. When we had fished the entire day and caught nothing, a friend of mine encouraged me to try a brand-new muskie lure. I'd never quite seen a lure like this one. It was as big around as a broom handle, jointed in the middle, covered with hooks, and extremely heavy. After attaching the lure, I tried casting it out, only to lose my balance and fall backward into the boat. It was both embarrassing and hilarious to watch as I tried to recover.

No sooner did the lure hit the water than the water around it boiled. I had, in fact, hooked my first muskie. The fight was on, and I was hooked, too...on the experience. I finally got the muskie to the boat and realized that I had managed to catch a fish that was over thirty inches long. What a thrill!

I also learned a valuable lesson. The lure that I used was made for muskie. You couldn't catch bream or crappie or even a large-mouth bass on it. After an exhausting day of trying everything else, the lure worked. It was designed to catch muskie, and that's exactly what it did. It had fulfilled its purpose.

Do you realize that you, too, were designed for a specific purpose? God created you to fulfill the specific purpose that He has just for you. In Psalm 139:14 and 16 it says:

> I praise you because I am fearfully and wonderfully made; your works are wonderful, I know that full well...your eyes saw my unformed body. All the days ordained for me were written in your book before one of them came to be. (NIV)

God prepared all the days of your life before you even lived one of them. He designed you on purpose. We find our significance when we live out that purpose for which God created us. If you don't know why God put you here, then your life can seem pretty meaningless. In fact, if you don't know your purpose, you'll never find significance.

God scheduled each day of your life before you even began to breathe. That's how much you matter to Him. He wants you to spend eternity with Him. He also wants your life here to count for something.

The typical seventy-year lifespan is spent:

- Sleeping   23 years
- Working   16 years
- Watching TV   8 years
- Eating   6 years
- Traveling   6 years
- Recreation   4½ years
- Being sick   4 years
- Getting dressed   2 years
- Pursuing God,   6 months
    including church

Most people miss the significance they can have in life because they don't break out of this pattern. Only by connecting with God, by coming to know Him through His Son, Jesus Christ, can you find the purpose for which you were made, and only then do you find significance.

I was within just a few casts of having to pack it in and head back to the lodge before trying that special lure which was designed for catching muskie. It fulfilled its purpose and proved its significance to me. Don't waste one second of your life before you find and live your purpose and experience the significance that comes with it. It is the only way to live life and know that you have made a difference...that your life really did matter.

That's the truth…about significance, in God's country

STARS

Psalm 19:1

The heavens declare the glory of God;

And the firmament shows His handiwork.

Psalm 147:4

He counts the number of the stars;

He calls them all by name.

I've always been fascinated by stars and the beauty of the night sky whenever I'm out in God's country. Whenever I'm somewhere in the wilderness, away from the artificial lights of our cities and towns, I always try to take a few moments to walk out and just stare at the night sky so that, once again, I can be captured by the majesty of God, who spoke not only our world, but also the stars, into existence.

Scripture quite frequently speaks about the significance of the stars. Genesis 1:14 says that God put "lights in the firmament of the heavens to divide the day from the night; and let them be for signs and seasons, and for days and years." In other words, God gave us the stars as signs, or symbols, of His interaction with man.

We're told that a Hebrew father could walk out on a starlit night, start from one horizon to the other, and use the example of the stars to present the story of God and the gospel to his children. Psalm 19:1 says, "The heavens declare the glory of God, And the firmament shows His handiwork." The skies illustrate God's handiwork.

Psalm 147:4 tells us that "He counts the number of the stars: He calls them all by name." God has named the stars and many of those names carry significance.

Christmas is truly the season of the star...the Star of Bethlehem. Matthew 2:1-2 says, "Now after Jesus was born in Bethlehem of Judea in the days of Herod the king, behold, wise men from the East came to Jerusalem, saying, 'Where is He who has been born king of the Jews? For we have seen His star in the East and have come to worship Him.'" A star...no, His star was seen by the wise men from the East. The Greek term used for these wise men is "Magi." They first appeared as a tribe of priests in the Babylonian empire. They believed in one god, and they worshiped him through the sacrifice of fire. It was believed they were descended from Noah's son, Shem, and served as a common ancestor of both the Jews and the Arabs. The Magi knew science, agriculture, and mathematics, and they exhibited extraordinary power. These men rose to prominence and became known as the king makers throughout the Persian and Babylonian empires. No Persian or Babylonian could become king without mastering the disciplines of the Magi and then being crowned by them.

During the Babylonian empire, something interesting happened to these Magi. The Jews had been conquered by Babylon, and they were brought to Babylon from their home in the Promised Land. One of those taken into captivity was a man named Daniel. Daniel, a man who honored the Lord, did something by God's power that none of the Magi of Babylon could do; he interpreted the king of Babylon's dream. Daniel 2:48 says that Daniel rose to such prominence that he became the chief administrator over all the wise men of Babylon. In other words, Daniel became chief of the Magi. Those Magi who came to see baby Jesus were part of a long tradition of the Magi who had been taught by Daniel. Just as a Hebrew father could teach his children the wonderful story of God reaching out to man through the stars, no doubt Daniel taught those same lessons to the wise men of the East. When the star appeared announcing the birth of Jesus, they understood exactly what was happening because Daniel had taught them. Matthew 2:11 tells us that when these wise men found Jesus, they "fell down and worshiped Him." They fully understood who Jesus was. Coming from Babylon and Daniel's leadership, they knew that Jesus was God come to earth. Through Daniel, the Magi had preserved the message of redemption, drawn on the canvas of the sky.

Ancient tradition tells us that Daniel taught the Magi in Babylon to look for the star of the Messiah, His star, to appear in the constellation Coma, right at the point of the Child on the Virgin's lap. When the star

> The star of glory moved and stood above the Christ.

appeared, that meant that the Messiah, the Christ, had arrived. It's interesting that in both the Old and New Testament, Christ is called "the Star." Numbers 24:17 says, "A Star shall come out of Jacob." Revelation 22:16 calls Jesus "the Bright and Morning Star."

The light that appeared in the constellation Coma, I believe, was more than just a star. I believe it was God's glory, the same glory that guided the children of Israel through the wilderness and filled the tabernacle. The reason I say that is because Matthew 2:9 says, "and behold, the star which they had seen in the East went before them, till it came and stood over where the young Child was." The star of glory moved and stood above the Christ. If ancient tradition is true, it's a beautiful picture: the glory of God appears as a light at the point of the Infant in the constellation Coma and then moves from heaven to earth to stand above the Christ Child. It's a graphic picture of the Son of God, leaving heaven to come to earth.

Daniel obviously did a wonderful job training the wise men as to who Jesus would be because the scripture tells us in Matthew 2:11, "they presented gifts to Him: gold, frankincense, and myrrh." Gold depicted the royalty of Jesus. Frankincense was used in the temple as incense for God, and only God was meant to receive it. How did these Gentiles from Babylon know that frankincense was meant only for God? Daniel must have taught them. How did they know that this Baby was God? Daniel taught them to look for His star, the star that would announce the coming of the Son of God. They also presented Him with myrrh, which was used to embalm bodies. It carried the fragrance of death. They even recognized that Jesus must die. How did these wise men know all of this? Daniel taught them to study the stars, to see and grasp the symbols of God's interaction with man.

The stars tell the story of the majesty of our Lord. His star, the star of the Messiah, announced His birth. The next time you're standing in God's country on a crisp, clear, starlit night, look up and be amazed and thank God for the gift of His Son Jesus.

That's the truth...about stars, in God's country.

LIVING YOUR PURPOSE

Matthew 6:33

But seek first the kingdom of God and His righteousness, and all these things shall be added to you.

The first men to see the wild turkey of North America were Spanish explorers in the sixteenth century. They actually brought some turkeys back to Spain around 1519 and began to domesticate them. The turkeys adapted well to life in Europe, and by 1530 were found throughout Germany. They later spread to England, where over a century later Englishmen loaded turkeys on their ships bound for new settlements in America to provide food for the settlers, causing the turkey to come full circle.[1]

The turkey helped the early settlers, the Pilgrims in particular, survive the difficult winters. Wild turkeys were abundant in America and served as a major source of food for the Native Americans. They also utilized the feathers of the turkey for ornaments and the sharp spurs on the feet of the turkeys for arrowheads. Due to the contribution it made during the settlement of this country, Benjamin Franklin recommended that the turkey be adopted as the national bird for the United States.

You may be thinking, that is more information than I ever wanted to know about turkeys. What's the deal? Well, being an outdoorsman, I simply have to indulge my fascination with turkeys at certain times of the year. When spring comes, most hunters I know count down the days until the beginning of turkey season. By late spring most have already bagged their turkeys and are still telling their stories of the hunt.

The great challenge of turkey hunting is that you're trying to get the male turkey (called a tom, or a jake, if he is very young) to do something that is totally unnatural. A male turkey lives with purpose. Weeks before mating season begins, the male turkey concentrates on feeding. The more it feeds, the more it develops what is known as a breast sponge, made up of a mass of thick cellular tissue. When mating season begins, the male turkey has stored enough food so that it can now focus on its next purpose–ensuring healthy offspring for the next generation.

For a male turkey to have a successful mating season, he will establish his dominance over a particular region and attract the female, or hen turkeys, to him in order to mate. He will face challenges from young jakes, but strength and experience allow the older turkeys to out-battle the young jakes until the older toms pass their prime. When a hunter uses a call to mimic a hen turkey, he is attempting to get the tom to not wait for the hen to come to him, but to leave his purpose and go to the hen. Hence, the great challenge of turkey hunting: in order to harvest a tom, you must get him to abandon his purpose.

This story's application to life is obvious. You and I are also created with a purpose. In fact, God uniquely made you with a purpose that He gave to no one else. Finding and living that purpose is really what life is all about. Developing the discipline to stick with that purpose keeps us from wasting our lives. In his book, *The Purpose Driven Life*, Rick Warren makes the statement that "The greatest tragedy is not death, but life without purpose."[2]

Realizing this fact causes us to face two crucial questions:

(1) How do I find my purpose?

(2) How do I keep from leaving my purpose?

The answer to both of those questions can be found in one simple passage of scripture, Matthew 6:33, "But seek first the kingdom of God and His righteousness, and all these things shall be added to you." In other words, put God first and He says, "I'll bring everything else into focus." Keep God first, and He will keep you from abandoning your purpose.

> Keep God first, and He will keep you from abandoning your purpose.

Just like the turkey who abandons his purpose, our greatest danger comes when we abandon the purpose for which we were created. God knows you better than anyone else. He sent His Son to set you free from anything that would hinder you from knowing Him and fulfilling the purpose for which He created you. I've often wondered what the very last thoughts of a tom turkey were just before he was harvested. If we leave God's purpose, like the turkey, it just may cost us more than we would really be willing to pay.

That's the truth…about God's purpose for you, in God's country.

CHALLENGES

Proverbs 27:19

As water reflects a face, so a man's heart reflects the man.

(NIV)

Recently, I had the opportunity to do something that was a great deal of fun but was also very challenging. I went sea duck hunting off the coast of Massachusetts at Cape Cod. While I've become accustomed to hunting ducks in Arkansas, this was a most unusual duck hunt. Instead of spreading the decoys and calling in the ducks as we do here in Arkansas, we spread the decoys on the open water and hoped that the sea ducks who were flying by would deviate from their path and come by our location. Then came the challenging part: we bounced up and down on ten-foot waves while we tried to shoot a duck flying by at what seemed to be supersonic speed. I realized that we had to hit the duck exactly right with our shot, or, because of its hardy nature, he would keep right on flying. I'll have to confess that I had many misses, but thoroughly enjoyed the afternoon; I was actually able to bag a drake eider, which will soon be gracing my wall.

As I sat in the boat and tried to compensate for the motion of the waves, as well as the speed of the ducks that we were trying to bag, I realized that this particular hunt was a tremendous parable for life. We all face challenging situations. For some, it can be habits that need to be broken; for others, it may involve relationships, finances, or even attitudes that we have embraced that need to be addressed. Ask yourself in what area of your life do you face challenges right now? Is it the pace of your life? Are you excessively worrying? Are you holding on to the past? Are you struggling with an addiction? Have your expectations not been met in a relationship? Do you feel a need to control others?

How do we compensate for those things in life that toss us up and down and for these circumstances that fly by us at alarming speeds? The scripture says this: "Therefore do not worry about tomorrow, for tomorrow will worry about itself. Each day has enough trouble of its own" (Matthew 6:34 NIV).

We can only give attention to what's happening right now. God will help us deal with what's coming up. Your challenges were not created in a day, and you won't make the changes you need to make overnight to deal with them. Thank God for each challenge you face, and deal with one challenge at a time. You can't change thirty things in your life at once, so focus on that one thing you can change, on that one challenge you can meet. Ask God which challenge you need to work on first.

Have you heard the saying, "How do you eat an elephant? One bite at a time." When you face your challenges, you have to break them down into bite-sized pieces. When you get up in the morning, ask God: Will you help me deal with this one challenge today? It may involve controlling your temper; you may need to forgive someone, or it may mean eating less or having a positive attitude. For some, dealing with that challenge today may be too big a bite. You may need to say: God, help me deal with this challenge for the next hour, or even just the next thirty minutes.

As those eiders came in, I recognized that they were coming at me faster than I had anticipated. As the flock flew by, I had to pick out one duck to focus on, just as we must focus on that one thing that needs to be changed in our lives. Proverbs 3:7 says it this way: "Do not be wise in your own eyes; Fear the LORD and depart from evil."

When we learn to rely on God's power, when we are willing to associate with the right people, and when we realize that facing those challenges begins by changing how you address them, then we know we are actively facing life's challenges.

We can make three very real mistakes in regard to our behavior in facing the challenges of life:

(1) We try to change our behavior first...However, we must first change our thinking, which changes our beliefs, which changes our attitudes, which, finally, changes our behavior.

(2) We wait for God to change our circumstances...more often, God wants to change us more than He wants to change our circumstances.

(3) We wait for circumstances to change our behavior. That just doesn't work.

Ultimately, the greatest challenges we face are not the circumstances around us, but those in our own heart. Proverbs 27:19 says it this way: "As water reflects a face, so a man's heart reflects the man" (NIV). In other words, just as you can see the reflection of your face outwardly in a pool of water, so a man's heart reveals what he really is.

When I was hunting sea ducks, it wasn't long before I began to gain the confidence that I could really meet this challenge, and soon that confidence became reality. I not only met the challenge, but I took a banded drake eider. For duck hunters, that's the equivalent of hitting a home run. The challenge had been met; the victory had been won. I had figured out the right thing to do, and I just kept doing it until I had faced the challenge of my performance.

We change our lives as we consistently do the right thing. However, we should never fall into the trap of thinking that God isn't going to love us until we finish facing our challenges. God looks at us right now, wherever we are in the process of facing our challenge, and says, "I love you and I want to help you." God wants to meet with you and help you face the challenges of your life. He wants to help you change, and He will if you let Him. That is why He sent His Son Jesus Christ. Jesus came to face the challenges we face so that He could sympathize with us, and, ultimately, deliver us from those challenges. Trusting your life and your challenges to Him is the greatest victory of all.

That's the truth…about facing challenges, in God's country.

CHANGES

Isaiah 43:18-19a
Do not remember the former things,
Nor consider the things of old.
Behold, I will do a new thing,
Now it shall spring forth;
Shall you not know it?

I am a fortunate man. You see, my wife Janice is not only my best friend, but she is also my hunting companion. For years she and I have hunted pheasant, quail, and other game birds together, and she is quite a wing shot. Several years ago, for our anniversary, she asked for a 20-gauge over-and-under shotgun to use on our frequent bird hunting trips. Yes, I am a fortunate man, indeed.

It didn't surprise me this year that Janice decided she also wanted to try her hand at deer hunting. While she was quite proficient with a shotgun, she had never fired a rifle; so prior to the start of the modern gun season for deer, we spent a Saturday afternoon helping her become acquainted with shooting a rifle. She did quite well.

We headed for southern Illinois, just outside the Shawnee National Forest, where we were planning a hunt in conjunction with our television program, *Adventure Bound Outdoors*. Early the next morning, Janice was in a deer stand with one of our cameramen while I was in another stand. Suddenly, at about 8:20 a.m., I heard a rifle shot in the direction of my wife's stand. I received a call on the walkie-talkie that a deer was down, and I headed in her direction.

What I found absolutely shocked me. The first time Janice had ever fired a rifle at a deer, she had harvested a seventeen point, 250-pound buck that had over a twenty-inch antler spread. To those of you who are outdoorsmen, you will understand that this is like hitting a hole-in-one the first time you swing a golf club. I stood there in awe and amazement as I realized my wife had just killed a deer bigger than any I had ever had the opportunity to bag. I was greatly humbled.

As I walked away from the deer, I asked Janice what she wanted to do with it. Her response was, "We'll have it mounted." I then asked her where we would hang it, since I had to hang all my trophies at the office instead of at the house. She responded we would hang it at the house. I asked her why she could hang hers at the house when I had never been able to hang my trophies at the house. She replied, "Because you've never harvested one this big before."

I was sufficiently humbled, and I realized that something new had occurred in our family. Janice is now hopelessly hooked. My life has changed forever...for the better. Since Janice is my best friend, it will be something new to have her participating in all of my outdoor pursuits. Things have changed.

Have you noticed that life is a constant series of changes? For those of us who have a personal relationship with God through Jesus Christ, we have the privilege of going on a journey with Him through our lives. The Bible says it this way in Isaiah 43:18-19a:

Do not remember the former things,
Nor consider the things of old.
Behold, I will do a new thing,
Now it shall spring forth;
Shall you not know it?

God basically tells us not to get in a rut. Don't expect things to always stay the same. God always does something new, exciting, and adventurous. The question that needs to be asked is, "Will you be part of it?" There are many people in life who refuse to get into the flow of what God does and the changes He wants to bring, not only in their lives, but also in the circumstances around them. While those changes may appear difficult or even painful, if we're cooperating with God, we know they will be for our good. At times those changes will be joyful, like sharing yet another outdoor activity with your best friend.

Remember that changes will happen. Let God direct the changes in your life so that you can stay on track with Him and experience the adventure of living life outside the ruts.

That's the truth...about changes, in God's country.

PREJUDICE

James 2:8-9

If you really fulfill *the* royal law according to the Scripture, *"You shall love your neighbor as yourself,"* you do well; but if you show partiality, you commit sin, and are convicted by the law as transgressors.

This past deer season, I was sitting in a deer stand when I saw one of the most unusual sights I've ever seen in the outdoors. Since we weren't filming for *Adventure Bound Outdoors* that day, I didn't even take my gun, simply because we don't want to harvest a deer without being able to get it on film for the program. I just love being in the outdoors and thought this would be a great time to relax and see some of God's creation.

I will never forget what happened that day. Suddenly, a flash of white darted through the woods off to my left. As I carefully turned my head, a beautiful albino doe stepped out of the woods and into the clearing below me. She began to graze nonchalantly across the clearing when a large, seven-point buck appeared on the opposite side of the clearing. He, too, began grazing until he saw the albino doe, which was now standing in the midst of four other does, quietly munching on the grass. Suddenly, the buck lowered his head and charged into the middle of the group of does, hitting the albino doe so hard that he knocked her over. She jumped up and scampered off in the direction from which she had come.

For the next thirty minutes I watched as the doe kept trying to re-enter the clearing, only to be charged by the buck. Finally, the doe gave up, and I last glimpsed her walking off alone through the forest. I had just witnessed my first experience with prejudice in God's country. I'm sure wildlife biologists could give us many reasons as to why the buck attacked the doe, but the bottom line is, she was different, and he didn't want her around.

While I may have never seen an act of prejudice in God's country before, I have witnessed it among people. My wife and I grew up in South Carolina during the 1960s and 1970s, when the civil rights movement was gaining momentum and integration had become the rule of the day. I was in the seventh grade when my school was integrated by one lone African-American girl.

I will always remember that first day when she enrolled in our school. The parking lot of the school was covered with fathers, some toting shotguns, some cursing loudly, and others simply sitting on the hoods of their cars, waiting to see what was going to happen. The police were there too and were able to maintain order. Inside the school, however, I watched as a seventh-grade African-American girl was kicked, pushed, shoved, had books knocked out of her hands, and was even tripped. I remember telling myself, "She won't be back tomorrow." But she came back. Day after day she returned, quietly accepting the abusive treatment and never seeking to retaliate. She sat alone at lunch; she walked alone down the halls; she sat in the back corner of each of the classrooms, and no one spoke to her. I wish

I could say I quickly rose to her defense, but I didn't. I just quietly watched. At the end of the first six weeks of school, she made her statement. By simply doing her schoolwork and doing it well, she had risen to the top of our class. Now I was intrigued.

One day, after a passing football player had knocked the books out of her hands, I watched as she quietly picked them up and walked into the lunchroom. I could stand it no longer. I walked over, took a seat beside her, and said, "I need to ask you a question. How can you handle all the abuse that is being heaped on you without retaliating or even seeming to get angry?" Her response changed my life. She said, "Because Jesus wouldn't have me get angry. He loves the people who mistreat me as much as He loves me." Needless to say, I was stunned. You see, I too, claimed to be a Christian. In fact, I was the leader of the Christian club in our class. It had never occurred to me that she also knew the Lord.

I would like to think that prejudice died in me on that day. In all honesty, it's still dying as I learn more about the love that Jesus has for all His people. The Bible says it this way in James 2:8-9: "If you really fulfill *the* royal law according to the Scripture, *'You shall love your neighbor as yourself,'* you do well; but if you show partiality, you commit sin, and are convicted by the law as transgressors."

The phrase "show partiality," in the original language, literally means, *to* "receive somebody's face." In other words, this means to receive somebody at face value, to size up someone based on superficial or external criteria. We simply have no right to show favoritism toward someone or to reject someone based on their race or heritage.

In Acts 17:26, Paul, preaching to the skeptics at Athens, said,

"And He has made from one blood every nation of men to dwell on all the face of the earth...." The color of someone's skin does not determine that person's value with God, nor should it with us. Does the church really understand this? If so, then why is the most segregated hour in our culture the hour of worship on Sunday morning?

That's the truth...about prejudice, in God's country.

TROPHIES

John 14:6

Jesus answered, "I am the way and the truth and the life. No one comes to the Father except through me." (NIV)

Hunters, especially those who hunt the bigger game, often use a common phrase: "That's a wall hanger." It means the animal harvested has a quality worthy of mounting as a trophy on the hunter's wall. Hunters love to display their trophies. In all honesty, I have a few of my own that I enjoy showing off.

I have a friend in another state who is quite a hunter. He has mounts of animals from all over the world. My friend's trophies have seen their share of hardships. Several years ago, my friend's home was destroyed by a tornado. He was able to salvage and repair all of his trophy wall mounts, some at considerable expense. Then, just a few years ago, my friend's house burned to the ground, destroying everything, including his costly wall mounts.

As he and his wife walked through the rubble of what had been their home, my friend noticed a glass eye in the charred remains of his den. It was all that was left of his once impressive collection of hunting trophies. As he rolled the glass ball around with his shoe, his wife walked over and commented, "Those trophies weren't very permanent, were they?" That comment caused my friend to begin evaluating what really was permanent in his life. After much thought, he came to the conclusion that what really mattered in his life was not the stuff he surrounded himself with, but the relationships he had, which no tornado or fire could steal from him. Those were his true trophies.

That's exactly what the Bible teaches. The most important trophies in life are not those things we hang on our walls or even the walls we hang them on. The trophies that matter most can be summed up in one word: relationships. The most important trophy is the love we share with others. That is, by the way, exactly what Jesus taught.

Someone asked Jesus on one occasion,

> "Teacher, which is the greatest commandment in the Law?" Jesus replied: "'Love the Lord your God with all your heart and with all your soul and with all your mind.' This is the first and greatest commandment. And the second is like it: 'Love your neighbor as yourself.' All the Law and the Prophets hang on these two commandments."
> (Matthew 22:37-40 NIV)

When all is said and done, and we find ourselves standing before the Creator of all things, He will not ask us to show Him our list of accomplishments, our accumulated stuff, or even our prize trophies. He will ask us about our relationships. First, do we know Him? Do we love Him? The only way we establish a love relationship with our

Creator is through His Son Jesus.

John 14:6 says, "Jesus answered, 'I am the way and the truth and the life. No one comes to the Father except through me'" (NIV).

> Did we form relationships with others that reflected our relationship with Him?

Jesus is the only way we can establish a relationship with the God who made the great outdoors and us.

God will also ask us about our relationships with others. Did we love others? Did we form relationships with others that reflected our relationship with Him? Those shared relationships are the permanent trophies of this life. In discussing the sum total of our lives, the Bible says:

> For no one can lay any foundation other than the one already laid, which is Jesus Christ. (*Jesus is how we come to know the God of the great outdoors*). If any man builds on this foundation using gold, silver, costly stones, wood, hay or straw, his work will be shown for what it is, because the Day will bring it to light. It will be revealed with fire, and the fire will test the quality of each man's work. If what he has built survives, he will receive his reward. If it is burned up, he will suffer loss; he himself will be saved, but only as one escaping through the flames. (I Corinthians 3:11-15 NIV)

In other words, once we come to know Jesus, our relationship with him becomes the foundation of our lives. Great loss results if we spend the energy and effort of our lives emphasizing the temporary trophies of life. Great rewards result if we spend our lives building relationships that no fire can destroy. Those are the trophies that matter.

My friend and I have come to a conclusion. Since it all begins with our relationship with Jesus, a relationship which happens by God's grace and which involved God sending His Son Jesus to go to the cross for us, we are trophies ourselves, trophies of the grace of God.

Ephesians 2:6-8 says, "And God raised us up with Christ...in order that...he might show the incomparable riches of his grace...For it is by grace you have been saved...."

I have been saved by His grace. I am forever a trophy of God's grace, and that's a privilege I'll have forever.

That's the truth...about trophies, in God's country.

WILD HOGS AND MEAN PEOPLE

Proverbs 29:11
A fool vents all his feelings,
But a wise *man* holds them back.

You can't live in Arkansas for very long without realizing how important the Razorbacks are. A traditional part of being from Arkansas involves attending an athletic event for the University of Arkansas and "calling the hogs." What is it about these razorbacks, or wild hogs, as they are commonly known in the outdoors? The Vanderbilt family first introduced the Russian boar into the U.S. in Western North Carolina and Eastern Tennessee. The Vanderbilts were railroad barons who were interested in providing their wealthy friends with yet another hunting option. They first released these ferocious animals into the area around Biltmore House in Asheville, North Carolina, near the Smokey Mountains.

Because these wild hogs repopulate so rapidly, with as many as 10-14 born per litter, they soon increased their habitat at a rapid rate and began to spread west. They began interbreeding with feral hogs, domesticated hogs that had reverted to the wild. Russian boars and feral hogs are practically indistinguishable. The ridge of stiff hair running up their backs gives these wild hogs their popular name, razorback. Over thirteen national park services now report that they have large populations of wild hogs, making the razorback the most prolific large wild mammal in the U.S.

These hogs are noted for their aggressive behavior. In fact, if you find yourself hunting in an area where there are lots of wild hogs, keep your eyes open. They have been known to attack dogs and people. These hogs love the darkness. One reason their sense of smell is so good and their eyesight so bad is because they are nocturnal. They are also, however, very intelligent and downright mean. It's almost as if they have a chip on their shoulder. Their tusks are razor-sharp, and it is imperative that you be cautious when encountering them in the outdoors because they *will* attack.

I would much rather encounter a bear while hunting than a wild hog. It's almost as if these hogs are mad at the world and anybody that gets in their way. I guess that makes them an appropriate mascot for the University of Arkansas. Wherever they go, and whatever they do, they just always seem ready to explode in anger.

I've known some people like that, people who are just downright mean. They quickly attack and slash, hurting other people and destroying other people's dreams, goals, and even lives. What would cause a person to allow anger to dominate their lives? The Bible says in Proverbs 14:16: "A wise *man* fears and departs from evil, but a fool rages and is self-confident." I like the way *The Message* paraphrases that verse when it says: "The wise watch their steps and avoid evil. Fools are headstrong and reckless."

A person who lets anger dominate them definitely becomes

"headstrong and reckless." In fact, they're just plain foolish. Proverbs 29:11 says: "A fool vents all his feelings, but a wise *man* holds them back."

A person can be so foolish that they lash out at people around them and at the very people they love. Buried anger is often the hidden killer in many families, just waiting to destroy relationships and create an unhealthy atmosphere.

To use an outdoor illustration, a family is often like putting a skunk and a turtle together. A skunk lets you know where you stand – they're aggressive. When this type of person gets upset, they'll stink up the whole place. But a turtle will go into his shell. This type of person tends to withdraw, back off and be passive. It's amazing how skunks tend to marry turtles. Is there an alternative to being one or the other? Yes, there is. You can either move against people in anger, like a skunk, away from people in fear, like a turtle, or with people in love.

> The idea is to express anger in appropriate ways, in ways that benefit you and your family.

When you talk about resolving anger in your family, in your relationships at work, or with friends, don't try to eliminate anger, because you can't. Try to express anger in appropriate ways, in ways that benefit you and your family. This is essential for healthy relationships.

The Bible not only tells us that a fool gives full vent to his anger, like a skunk, but it also says that a fool will say in his heart that there is no God (Psalm 14:1). I think a lot of the anger that some people so readily display has to do with their relationship with God. They forget that He made them, that He cares about them, and whatever has made them angry or upset is under His control. Maybe you've run into someone that is perpetually angry, attacking people like an angry wild hog. Possibly you've even been hurt by someone like that. It's so easy to be damaged by those people who walk around being upset all the time. Don't let them ruin your life.

The reason they are so angry is that they have ignored God. They have decided that they are going to live life their way, and in the process, they have become hurt, frustrated, or even afraid, causing them to give full vent to their anger. Don't let them cause you to become like them. You don't have to be angry. Hurt people hurt people. You can break the cycle.

You don't have to ignore God; God didn't ignore you. He sent His Son Jesus just for you because He cares about you. He loves you very much, and because He loves you, He wants you to live in His joy, not in anger. Perhaps you know someone who has knocked the props out from under you with their angry attacks. Remember, God is in control, and He loves you, and you can cast all your cares on Him. I Peter 5:7 says: "…casting all your care upon Him, for He cares for you."

While you're in God's country, don't get caught off guard by a wild hog, and while you're living your life, don't get caught off guard by a mean person. Just smile, remind them that God loves them, and refuse to be infected with their bitterness. Those are some of the best lessons I know for surviving in life.

That's the truth…about wild hogs and mean people in God's country.

THE PATH OF LIFE

Psalm 33:5
He loves righteousness and justice;
The earth is full of the goodness of the LORD.

Several years ago on a trip to Alaska, my wife and I had the privilege of visiting the spawning grounds of the salmon. I was intrigued to learn about the remarkable capacity that this fish has to find its way home. Once the eggs hatch in the spawning ground, the small salmon will stay in the area and feed until they grow to about four to eight inches. Then they will begin the long trek downstream to the ocean, pausing at the mouth of the river to adjust to the salt water. For the next one to four years, the salmon will stay in the ocean and travel thousands of miles, frequently swimming as many as twenty to sixty miles a day.

The urge to return to their freshwater home occurs suddenly and with great intensity in each of the salmon. When they feel this need to return to the place where they were hatched, the salmon immediately begin navigating to the mouth of the river from which they came. Relying on the position of the moon and the sun, the salmon can swim directly upstream to the place where they began their lives.

The remarkable capacity of the salmon to find its spawning ground is legendary. The thousands of rivers, inlets, harbors and bays, do not daunt the salmon in their drive to return home. They also have legendary tenacity. Frequently, they will attempt to leap up waterfalls, pressing on in the face of huge obstacles and numerous predators. They just simply know where they're going. In other words, there are no confused salmon.

The tedious upstream journey may take as long as six months while the salmon struggle against the current and go without food the entire time. Once they arrive at their spawning grounds, the salmon lay their eggs, die, and the cycle begins again. That the salmon can discern exactly how to return to their spawning ground is nothing short of amazing. They just simply know what direction to take.

Do you sometimes feel that we live in a world that has lost its ability to know which path to take, the ability to even tell right from wrong? The Bible teaches us that God puts a conscience in everyone. Some refuse to listen to their conscience or harden it so they can no longer sense its guidance. God put a conscience within each of us to guide us by His goodness, much like the salmon experience the guidance of God in creation.

The Bible says in Psalm 33:5, "The earth is full of the goodness of the LORD." Everywhere you look, if your eyes are trained to discern it, you can see God's goodness. The conscience that He places within us connects us to the goodness of God around us and helps guide us in the paths that we should take in life.

Are you confused about which way to go or what path to take? Someone has defined God's will as what we would want for ourselves if we could see everything, know everything, and understand everything. *USA Today*, several years ago, did a survey in which they asked Americans to respond to this question: "Given an opportunity to get a direct and clear response from God, what question would you ask Him?" The clear winner in the survey, by a huge majority, was: "What is Your will, God, for my life?"

There's a great misconception about God's will for our lives. We often think we must find it. But you don't find God's will for your life; it finds you. If I want one of my sons to do something for me, I tell him what I want him to do. I don't expect him to guess what it is. It is not my son's responsibility to figure out what I want him to do; it is my responsibility to reveal it to him. In the same way, it is God's responsibility to reveal His will to us; it is our responsibility to do it.

> But you don't find God's will for your life; it finds you.

Psalm 37:4 says, "Delight yourself also in the LORD, and He shall give you the desires of your heart." In other words, when you allow God, not the world, to shape you, then God places within you the desires He wants you to have in your heart. You start wanting what God wants for you. God will lead you by the desire He has placed within your heart as He shapes your life. As you delight in the Lord, you sensitize yourself to the conscience He has placed within you and gain the ability to choose what is right over what is wrong. As God shapes the wants of your heart so that you want His will, you begin to discern the path that God wants you to take in your life. You not only do what is good, but you do His will, and God directs your life.

If God can direct a salmon to its spawning ground, He can guide you. Proverbs 3:5-6 says it best: "Trust in the LORD with all your heart, and lean not on your own understanding. In all your ways acknowledge Him, and He shall direct your paths." God will direct your path by your conscience and your desires as you acknowledge Him in all you do. Trust Him, and try Him; you'll see that He is good.

That's the truth...about the path of life, in God's country.

NOTES

THIRSTING FOR GOD

1. Eldredge, John. *Wild at Heart*. Nashville: Thomas Nelson Incorporated, 2001. pg. 5.

GETTING OUTDOORS

1. Culbreath, Judson. "Making Mud Pies," *Reader's Digest*. July 2005. rd.com

2. Ibid

3. Ibid

4. Ibid

5. Ibid

BELONGING

1. *Character Sketches*, Volume 1. Rand McNally and Company: Institute in Basic Youth Conflicts, Incorporated, 1976. pg. 107-108.

ENCOURAGEMENT

1. *Character Sketches*, Volume 1. pg. 158-160.

FOCUSING ON WHAT MATTERS
1. *Character Sketches*, Volume 2. 1978. pg. 29-33.

SALT
1. Scott, Jack Denton. "Let's Give Salt a Fair Shake," *Reader's Digest*. November 1988. pg. 17-19..

FRIENDSHIP
1. *Character Sketches*, Volume 2. pg. 107.

2. Ibid

3. Ibid

LIVING YOUR PURPOSE
1. *Character Sketches*, Volume 1. pg. 153.

2. Warren, Rick. *The Purpose Driven Life*. Grand Rapids: Zondervan, 2002. pg. 30.

PREJUDICE
1. *Character Sketches*, Volume 1. pg. 209

2. *Character Sketches*, Volume 1. pg. 210

ABOUT THE AUTHOR

Dr. Chuck McAlister and his wife, Janice, are avid hunters. In 1996, as a ministry of his church, Chuck launched *Adventure Bound Outdoors*, a nationally syndicated Christian hunting program, which has averaged 300-400 salvation decisions per month. He serves as senior pastor of the Church at Crossgate Center in Hot Springs, Arkansas.

Chuck and Janice have two sons, Chris (who is married to Brandi) and Jeff, plus three very special granddaughters, Ashlynn, Madilynn, and Braelynn.

Also Available From

THE OUTDOOR BIBLE®
SPORTSMAN'S EDITION – KJV
GOD'S COUNTRY® CAMOUFLAGE COVER

THE OUTDOOR BIBLE®
SPORTSMAN'S EDITION – KJV
MOTHWING™ CAMOUFLAGE COVER

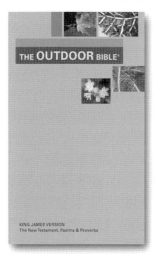

THE OUTDOOR BIBLE®
KJV – NT, PSALMS & PROVERBS

THE OUTDOOR BIBLE®
NAS UPDATED – NT